An Exploration Resource Usage in Interconnected Home Setups via an Connected Device Approach

Jamil Malik

An Exploration Resource Usage in Interconnected Home Setups via an Connected Device Approach

First Edition June 2025

Written by Jamil Malik

TABLE OF CONTENTS

CHAPTER NO.	TITLE	PAGE NO.

CHAPTER NO.	TITLE	PAGE NO.

LIST OF TABLES

TABLE NO.	TITLE	PAGE NO.

LIST OF FIGURES

FIGURE NO.	TITLE	PAGE NO.

LIST OF SYMBOLS AND ABBREVIATIONS

AODV	-	Ad Hoc On Demand Distance Vector
AOTDV	-	Ad Hoc Trust Based on Demand Distance Vector
ACO	-	Ant Colony Optimization
BPNN	-	Back Propagation Neural Network
BER	-	Bit Error Rate
CRN	-	Cognitive Radio Network
CPLNC	-	Cooperative Layer Network Coding
COMIC	-	Cost Optimization for Internet Control Multi homing
DSDV	-	Destination Sequenced Distance Vector
DSPV	-	Destination Sequenced Position Vector
DE	-	Differential Evolution
DDoS	-	Distributed Denial of Service
ERC	-	European Research Cluster
ETSI	-	European Telecommunication Standards Institute
IoT	-	Internet of Things
LEACH	-	Low Energy Adaptive Clustering Hierarchy
MDV	-	Multi Path Distance Vector
MAC	-	Multiple Access Control
PSTN	-	Public Switched Telephone Network
QoS	-	Quality of Service
SDN	-	Software Defined Network
SCTP	-	Stream Control Transmission Protocol
TCP	-	Transfer Control Protocol

UWB	-	Ultra Wide Band
UDP	-	User Datagram Protocol
WSN	-	Wireless Sensor Network

CHAPTER 1

INTRODUCTION

Wireless environment and multimedia plays a vibrant role in the contemporary networking technology which provides solutions to the limitations present in the wired environment. With this development, the Transfer Control Protocol (TCP) is transferred into Stream Control Transmission Protocol (SCTP) and is directly motivated by the Public Switched Telephone Network (PSTN) signalling messages across internet protocol.

1.1 BACKGROUND

The concept of multi homing is understood based on the IP terminology, since it describes communication node or host as multi homed because it can be accessed by multiple IP address. IP networks in today's world faces network failure and it needs a time to re-converge themselves to provide a new path. So routing plays a key role in multi homing in order to avoid the failure of paths in the network. Generally Multihoming is designed with TCP Protocol and if provides resilience to the network failures and provides fast recovery with minimum time and during this time the traffic is considered as black holed within the network. Stream controlled transmission protocol is not affected by network re-convergence term since the packet losses are identified immediately and it retransmits through another address based on the routing protocol suggestions. So this SCTP model provides faster recovery and better throughput. This can be implemented in the multiple interface networks to provide multipath communication through multiple IP address. Figure 1.1 illustrates a simple description about multi homing host. It consists of a single host and three interface lines such as N1, N2 and N3 with different IP address to ensure the multi homed model and in the host there will be a unique transport number that uses IP address as IP1, IP2 and IP3.

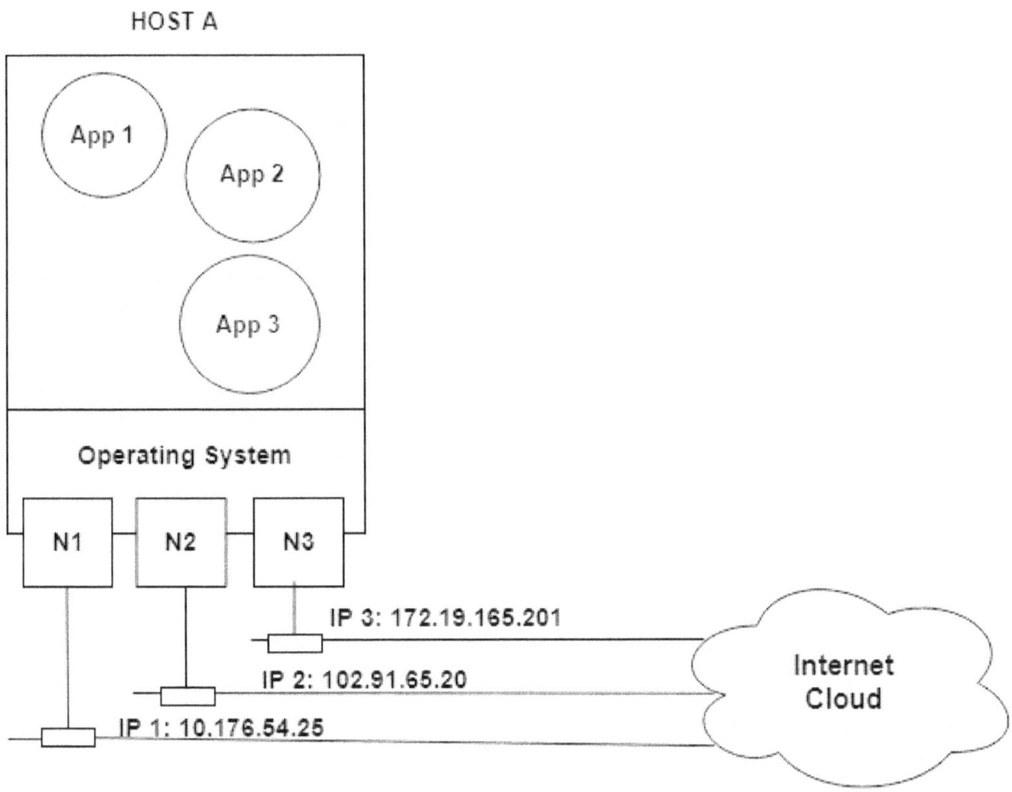

Figure 1.1 Multihomed host with multiple network interfaces

This multi home interfaces exchanges information from host to cloud and vice versa through this IP address and the secured path provided by the routing algorithm. Like TCP the SCTP also offers end to end communication for reliable deliver above the IP address based networks. It provides full duplex communication line called association for running the TCP without any loss function. The two major capabilities considered in designing the network as Multihomed host support and multiple stream support in association with multiple paths to achieve the path redundancy. To achieve fast failover from one path to other path a small interruption occurs in network service and this SCTP resolves that issues and supports multihoming model in Internet of Things environment.

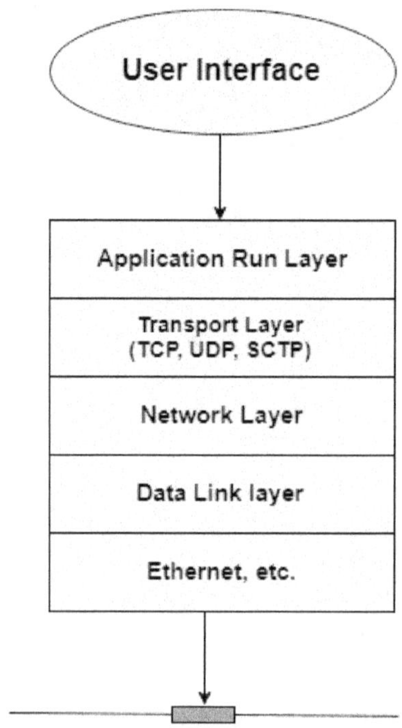

Figure 1.2 Reference Model of the SCTP

The essential need of SCTP over the wireless networks is to provide end to end transport service and transport layer of SCTP is shown in figure 1.2. It provides message oriented service between two communications and also describes their functionalities when failure occurs in the network.

1.2 MOTIVATION OF THESIS

Commercial applications and various data transfer applications need a quality oriented services to improve its robustness and the entire network performance. By varying the capacities and data utilization rates some applications does not satisfy with routing mechanism which is used in TCP and UDP since these layers are inadequate in performing large data. This motivates the development of SCTP in multi homing model along with the best routing protocol so that the recital of the system maintains its level and also increases the throughput. SCTP contains one or more building blocks called chunks for controlling the data at the time of congestion.

It uses a transmission sequence number for each protocol unit and also it provides acknowledgement like TCP. The motivation of multihoming in IoT is mainly based on the congestion control algorithms based on IEEE standard. This supports the multihoming model in transport layer by binding the IP address in the initial process itself. It allows multihomed data transfer from multiple sources and destinations based on parameters such as retransmission rate. Concurrent multipath transfer performs a host to destination data transfer model for end to end communication and also it increases the network throughput. It maintains a receiver to receive buffer and is communal across the various sub association flows in case of path failure.

Doubled and retransmission is performed in RTO and it increases the retransmission rate and also increases the buffer blocking duration in exponentially increased manner. This degrades the overall throughput if the packet loss occurs in an active path. This will not be used in data retransmission. The motivation of thesis is mainly focused in designing an efficient routing model to avoid path failure in the data transmission model by a redundant transmission path to ensure reliable communication. This motivation

(i) Provides efficient routing for reducing the data loss

(ii) Selecting the optimal model for routing

(iii) Increase the throughput and decrease the data transfer time.

This research work attempts to fulfil these needs, using neural network based routing model and an ant colony based optimization. This reduces the transfer rate because of utilizing the best and shortest path in retransmission if the node fails. Multi homing model and IoT information's are available in (Jongwook Lee *et al.* 2013) (Junfei Huang *et al.* 2017) (Oladayo Bello and Sherali Zeadally., 2016) (Liumeng *et al.* 2017)

1.3 OBJECTIVE OF THE THESIS

The quick development of wireless technologies and a secure end to end connection is essential for users. Thus it creates uncertain traffic loads in network and hence data transfer through suitable path in this dynamic network has different QoS characteristics. From the practical observations, multipath transfer and less path failure frequency are the two factors to be followed in heterogeneous networks.

The path failure affects the performance of system since the minor delay in each failure results into cumulative impact on file transfer thus it degrades the throughput of the network. The main objective of the thesis is to reduce the failure rates and improve the overall throughput. For achieving this a QoS based transmission path is identified and this path supports to carry redundant data in case of failure, until the path is recovered. This redundant path with redundant data acts as subsidiary path to overcome the path failure and reducing the packets drops. This dissertation introduces a new routing algorithm for multipath transmission in IoT which fulfils the needs and improves the overall performance.

1.4 CONTRIBUTION OF THESIS

The efficient routing model is used in the proposed system to support multihoming application in IoT environment using neural network and routing algorithms. This routing is essential in data transmission, path failure retransmission using transport layer model such as SCTP. This thesis proposed an optimized model in obtaining best route in the multihoming to achieve multiple data transfer over multiple paths. Due to network characteristics the data transfer uses a reordering scheme for the loss packet data and these results into throughput degradation.

Research finding states that in multihoming environment if the host uses two or more paths for data transmission than a buffer blocking problem will occur in the network. The IOT based ACO-MDV Algorithm is the contribution proposed in this thesis and incorporated in BPNN and SCTP layer.

The ACO-MDV basically consists of two findings for performance enhancement. They are,

a. Choosing an efficient Path for Redundant Transmission.

b. Determining the retransmission Period

1.4.1 Choosing an efficient Path for Redundant Transmission.

Research findings are used to observe the existing routing mechanisms and optimization models does not satisfy the requirements of the network and this causes interference in some cases. This research focused on providing an efficient routing model for redundant transmission. In order to ascertain that an experimentation model is used in the proposed model using Back propagation neural network and ant colony optimization model along with MDV algorithm. The result shows that the proposed model provides better results than the existing model and the system is employed for redundant transmission. The main aim of the subsystem is to obtain the suitable path among multiple transmission paths by supporting the path and exploiting the failure path. Each path in the network has unique characteristics and based on the quality of service and quality of path assed this is summarized for the following factors

- Retransmission time
- Congestion Rate
- Threshold value
- Loss rate

In the above parameter, priority is given into retransmission since it is essential in all the situations. The highest priority has strongest path since the retransmission is essential in the WSN and others are considered as low priority as a sequence.

- Initially an efficient path is choosing for highest priority and to choose the least prioritized path for next priority process.
- An effective optimization algorithm that overcomes the drawbacks in the multihoming host operations in IoT environment.

1.4.2 Determining the Retransmission Period

The multipath ACO-MDV algorithm in IoT environment observes the status of the network to assign the path priorities before the transmission starts. The main factor is used to identify the path failure and provide suitable path for the findings from the network. The internet traffic flow is dynamic in nature and it changes sequentially and this causes miss-prediction of network model. This has to be overcome by analysing the nature of path characteristics before the retransmission process occurs. Experimental results provide an appropriate time period as value for the proposed algorithm. Various files and based on various time intervals a failure processed in the network based on the dynamic characteristics in path allocation. This results dynamic path characteristics for equal and unequal interfaces even for failure and non failure conditions.

1.5 ORGANIZATION OF THE THESIS

The remainder of the thesis is organized as follows:

Chapter 2 presents a review of the relevant literature carried on the multihoming models and multicast models. Following this a survey of various implementations in IoT and its applications , routing algorithms, optimized routing methodologies and its limitations in the WSN environment is presented.

Chapter 3 presents the overall view of the multi homing and IoT. This chapter deals with the detailed analysis of multi homing concepts and its types, also a detailed discussion made on IoT and its applications to ensure the limitations and advantages present in combining the multihoming and IoT concept in the proposed research model.

In Chapter 4, ETSI-M2M Based Identification Schemes is discussed along with the modified architecture. IoT oriented heterogeneous networks and their identification scheme is discussed in this chapter based on the ETSI standard architecture. The result discusses the identifier formats in detail for the proposed model.

Chapter 5 discusses about secured routing protocol in multihoming IoT environment using neural network. A back propagation neural network is used in this chapter for obtaining a secure routing model for enhancing the performance of the entire system.

Chapter 6 deals with the optimization model of routing algorithm present in chapter 5. The neural network based routing produced a best routing scheme and this optimization makes the system better than the BPNN based routing. Ant colony based optimization model is used to predict the best routing model for the proposed research work integrated by MDV routing algorithm.

Chapter 7 summarizes and suggests the future scope of the work to be carried out as a continuation of this research.

CHAPTER 2

LITERATURE SURVEY

Internet of Things (IoT) is an embedded technology used to communicate or sense the data within the network or from other networks. Based on this definition the utilization of IoT is not limited to single field and it extend its hands in all research applications such as smart city, big data applications, medical and image processing areas and mainly in multipath communications.

2.1 INTRODUCTION

Multi homing and multiple access in the network has exponential growth in the heterogeneous networks because of the availability of the built in communication technological devices. In order to increase the dependability and performance of high end server's multi-homing is a long term technique used by the manufactures. Multi band services are adopted by the technologies to realize the multiple access network selection in today's heterogeneous networks. The mechanism which is used in the present scenario is based on the static policies and it doesn't require any input from the user side. Different networks and its process on heterogeneous networks have capabilities to establish a high performances communication and also to intricate applications based on its protocol configurations such as reliability, ubiquity, and flow distribution. This survey highlights the performance of Multihoming and IoT in various research works and also its merits and demerits by a comparison.

In order to exchange data from one terminal to other terminal this IoT uses sensors of various levels and fields to make the technical vision into real in the normal life. Based on this vision and ideas IoT needs to comprehend its terms in the research field as follows

1. Ubiquitous Network concept which is essentially used to focus on the communication at any point and any time concept.
2. Next generation network concept is used to highlight the advantages in the Internet of Things to form the platform for the future applications.

This research and discussions about various literatures discussed below can be grouped into four aspects with a minimum margin of variations in each category

- Multi-homing
- Various aspects in Multi-homing
- Internet of Things (IoT)
- Routing algorithms

2.2 MULTIHOMING RESEARCH ISSUES:

Multihoming was initially used in the wired networks and the co-existence of wireless network has renewed the concept because of its redundancy solution. The concept of multi-homing started with offloading concept which is used in load balancing, optimal distribution and also in concurrent multiple access network. The data offloading process was discussed in the literature in order to avoid overload in the end user experience. The three offloading key data is proposed based on the local IP Access, Selected IP, and IP Flow mobility.

(Aditya *et al.* 2008) discussed about the performance comparison of multi homing control in various network applications. The proposed architecture in the routing model overcomes the latency and intruder operations in the network and enhances the security of the network. **(Chung-Ming *et al.* 2010)** proposed a concurrent multipath transfer model to transmit data in multihomed networks with increased transmission speed. The important factor in the CMT over wireless networks based on the features such as path oriented streaming, handoff mechanisms. The error loss and the handoff loss are considered to reduce the receiver blockings in the proposed model.

(Li. X *et al.* 2010) reports a multipath routing model in a mobile ad hoc network. In mobile ad hoc network all the nodes acts as a routers and in an open environment it may affect due to the attacks and increased hazards. The proposed model uses on demand distance vector routing protocol for multipath routing and trust based ad hoc on demand distance vector is also proposed. Hop counts and trust values are used to evaluate the network and also a two dimensional evaluation provides shortest path to the users based on their needs. Experimental results provides a comparison which is used to obtain the difference between the AODV, AOTDV and a better result is obtained in the research through AOTDV with improved packet delivery ratio, less black hole and grey hole attacks.

(Miguel Camelo *et al.* 2011) discussed about the routing algorithms in multi objective mesh networks for improving the quality of services of network through optimization using multi objective evolutionary algorithm. Generally multiple objects conflicts with each other and it needs many traditional approximations to optimize the QoS parameters without conflicting to the other solutions. To improve the routing solution this model considers the essential parameters such as packet loss, delay and power consumption.

(Daniel Wallace *et al.* 2012) reports about the issues in stream control protocol in the multi homing model. If more than one device is use in the network to enhance the performance then the unused resources can be used as analternative access control networks. To improve reliability, throughput the transmission control protocol is essential and in particular stream control transmission protocol (SCTP) is used in the proposed model. Various research works are employed in the survey work to obtain the parameters of SCTP in the network.

(Jongwook Lee *et al.* 2013) proposed a cost minimized on demand video service for the heterogeneous wireless network in a multi homed terminal. Parameter estimation, threshold adjustment, compensation are the three factors mainly considered in the VoD stream. Based on the estimated parameter values markov decision process model is considered as an exponentially distributed value. To resolve this problems in markov model the proposed algorithm compensates the errors through continuous simulations and it is compared through statistical schemes.

(Romain Kuntz *et al.* 2013) report about the challenges and its solutions in the multihoming IPv6 mobile network. Since TCP is essential in multihoming mobility management this IPv6 had more benefits with multiple mobile routers. It provides a transparent end to end node multi homing system to enhance the performance. **(Donghyuk Han *et al.* 2014)** discussed about the multipath routing algorithm to overcome the end to end delay minimization. Proposed multipath routing has minimized network delay and its parameters are estimated based on the fractional Brownian motion. Co-operative game algorithm is incorporated in the system model to compute the average delay and optimal traffic distributions.

(Muhammad Ismail and Weihua Zhuang., 2014) discussed about the energy management system in a multi homing video transmission. Mobile terminals and call duration are analysed based on the statistical results obtained from the proposed model video encoding statistics. The energy consumption and its performance was analysed using simulation results over two bench marks and tradeoffs. **(Jianguo *et al.* 2015)** proposed an optimization model for internet content multi homing. Generally content service provides plenty of contents to the end users to ensure high performance in delivering data from one node to other nodes based on content distribution networks. The major contribution of content service is optimized in terms of cost in the proposed model. This cost optimization for internet content multi homing (COMIC) dynamically balances the loads in the networks.

(Quang-Doanh Vu *et al.* 2015) discussed about the efficient bandwidth and power allocation for multi homing networks. The proposed model uses multi homing network to transmit and receive data from multiple radio networks using air interface. **(Chuah *et al.* 2013)** also discusses about this energy efficiency, maximizes the quality of service of the network for all the available resources. This optimal solution facilitates into parameter free approach to develop a centralized algorithm for multipliers. To integrate the proposed model for obtaining the optimal solution convex program is used in the system. Greedy algorithm and sparsity based induced system is used in the simulation model to calculate the energy efficiency in the proposed model.

(Sai Qian Zhang *et al.* 2015) discussed about the routing algorithms in the multicast SDN. The services such as multimedia distribution and real time event monitoring involves in the multi cast concept. Virtualization concept is used in the proposed model to virtualize the infrastructures of the network and its software provides details regarding the functionality of the build equipment. **(Sandeep Kumar Singh *et al.* 2015)** reports about various internet multipath routing and its provisioning as a survey in the present scenario. Dominant path delivery and fulfilling the quality of service is a logical requirement in the wireless network for better resource utilization and reliability. In order to balance the data load in the network traffic this multipath helps through various protocols and also in the proposed model a mathematical description for challenges and issues are formulated at different internet layers.

(Satyam Agarwal *et al.* 2016) discussed about energy and cost aware video transmission in licensed cellular networks through cognitive multihoming. In order to minimize the transportation cost in the cognitive radio networks transmission rate and resource allocations are optimized. A comparison work is performed by the author in the research work against cognitive radio network to this proposed LCN. From the experimental results the performance of LCN is better than the CRN while maintaining the desired quality and energy consumptions.

(Junfei Huang *et al.* 2017) proposed a reliable multipath communication using under water sensor networks for the acoustic based applications. Forward error correction is performed in the proposed model using underwater sensor networks to achieve high performance. Multipath forward error correction is proposed in the research model using hamming code and Markov in model for enhancing the performance of efficiency and reliability of the network. Existing multipath communication models has more delay than this proposed model and it consumes only 20 -30% of energy with various bit error rates.

(Jiaxin *et al.* 2018) evaluates the performance of retransmission mechanism in heterogeneous communication system using fifth generation and 3GPP features. A mobile device with multiple interfaces uses this multipath connectivity to provide uninterrupted service to the users. This Multiple transmission control protocol (MPTCP) uses multipath parallel transmission to achieve high data delivery and denial of service attacks. Retransmission data causes unwanted expense to the network and this MPTCP retransmission mechanism which may cause buffer blocking by retransmits data over the same path can be avoided by using non congested path mechanism.

(Lei Xu *et al.* 2018) discussed about the power and bandwidth allocation process in a cognitive multi homing network. In cognitive heterogeneous networks during the uplink process the power allocation and bandwidth allotment is considered as issue since the joint power and bandwidth has constrains in the system model. For a secondary mobile terminal the minimum interference power is formulated based on the game framework. Nash bargaining solution is obtained from the optimal results obtained from bandwidth allocation algorithm. The proposed model finally implements the heuristic algorithm to reduce the complexity of the system and also to increase the spectrum efficiency.

(Runzi Liu *et al.* 2018) proposed a resource allocation model in heterogeneous wireless networks to obtain the energy efficient multi homed environment. The energy efficiency is formulated by an efficiency maximization problem along with the mixed integer non-linear optimization problem. For providing solution to this problem and also to reduce the computational complexity, continuity relaxation and dual Lagrange model is used in the proposed model. Experimental result in the proposed model uses two phase optimization model to achieve better results in computation and power efficiency and also less complexity.

2.3 RESEARCH IN INTERNET OF THINGS (IOT)

(Flammini *et al.* 2014) discussed about IoT and Cloud computing trends in the present technological world. Low cost and low power transceivers are used in the WSN for large scale and small scale applications. The main aim in the modern environment is to sample and collect all the information and process the same to improve its efficiency and reduce the resource consumptions. IoT has capability to provide such environment by joint together with cloud services. This cloud service is more flexible and powerful in computing services.

(Raja Vara Prasad Yerra *et al.* 2015) proposed a Multi-Hop wireless network in a dense traffic network as a part of IoT application to obtain the reliability and delay performance. IEEE 802.15.4 is used in the research work to obtain the behaviour of nodes and optimization parameters are obtained for the performance analysis. Active state length, packet length is considered for obtaining the reliability metrics.

(Oladayo Bello and Sherali Zeadally .,2016) discussed about internet of things as intelligent device to device communication model. Devices will communicate with the others through a centralized control centre in Multi-Hop manner. The proposed model has real time information collection model to provide an intelligent environment. The quality of information which is collected depends upon the networking standards and the connectivity between the resource terminals. The proposed model used D2D communication to achieve the IoT applications.

(Al-Ali *et al.* 2017) discussed about smart energy management system using big data analytics in IoT environment. Various Big data applications are present in the current scenario to enhance the features of heterogeneous networks. Hadoop and sun spark applications provides solution to the problems in the big data analytics and also is good in handling the data processing.

(Aviji *et al.* 2017) reports a secure end to end IoT solution model in the wireless heterogeneous networks. Several applications used this end to end solution such as medical, civil and other domestic domains. In each domain they have different requirements and challenges and in that data security is an important issue. Since this end to end secure solution in WSN provided network security and it works against attacks and other denial of services.

(Catalina *et al.* 2017) discussed about IoT applications in monitoring and reporting process such as smart homes and cities.WSN generally collects information and reports environment status through a gateway in the proposed model. The proposed model uses several distribution algorithms for detecting the mobile sink in the IoT infrastructure. WSNet simulator is used to analyse the performance of algorithm and this simulator is designed for event based wireless sensor networks.

(Fadi Al-Turjman *et al.* 2017) reports about the challenges in IoT data delivery applications in a multimedia sensor network. The proposed model uses multipath routing in the WSN to realize the real time constrains and is observed in simulation models. **(Jian Li *et al.* 2017)** discussed about the green computing IoT in the network to optimize the performance in coding based communication. The proposed model improves the network performance and also reduces the energy consumption using code based communication and reliable storage in the IoT. A polynomial time optimal storage allocation scheme is implemented in the proposed model using data center and failure probability values to improve storage allocation scheme.

(Jian Shen *et al.* 2017) proposed a routing model in WSN IoT to reduce the common constrains in the network model. Storage resources, computing resources are considered to maintain stable state in robust routing protocols. The proposed model uses energy efficient centroid based routing protocol for calculating the centroid position. An adaptive clusters and rotating clusters are used to find the position which is evenly distributed among the sensor nodes. Since this model has much number of nodes and in case of long distance communication energy consumption is considered as main factor and the residual energy is calculated using EECRP model. Simulation results highlights that the proposed model has better performance results in terms of life time and power consumption compared to LEACH, LEACH C models.

(Liumeng *et al.* 2017) proposed an energy efficient model in the IoT system using cluster based model. This model is used to improve the operational efficiency and reduce the power consumption. The problems in QoS and energy efficiency is considered as limitation in the existing model and a quantum particle swarm optimization model is used along with non dominated sorting genetic algorithm in the proposed model. To obtain optimal front end model this genetic algorithm is used and to achieve energy efficiency the QoS is considered in the proposed model.

(Mohammed Zaki Hasan *et al.* 2017) proposed an optimization model in the multipath routing IoT along with fault tolerance model. Particle swarm optimization based algorithm is proposed in the research model to reduce the issues in connectivity of objects and peoples. Routing multi swarm is used to select disjoint paths and fault tolerance levels which is considered as service parameter in selecting the multipath network. Experimental results are compared with canonical particle swarm optimization model to discuss that the PMSO has 88.45% of improvement over the CPSO.

(Antonio *et al.* 2018) proposed a dynamic algorithm for energy harvesting in IoT environment. The energy harvesting system guarantees the energy neutrality of the devices based on the proposed programming algorithm. In this model solar cells are used to harvest the energy and the algorithm finds the optimal solution gor the NP hard problem in a polynomial time. Experimentations are performed in various platforms such as Tmote, Arduino and raspberry PI on various situations and production rates.

(Asad *et al.* 2018) discussed about the IoT based model for software product line to support the multi objective system. Feature model and the binary pattern nested cardinally constrains considered in the proposed model to manage the features in the IoT network. The risk in IoT model due to its constraint violations, optimum feature combinations changes the multi objective IoT into a challenging module. Proposed model has heuristic paths to define the execution time and complexity. In the experimentations proposed model considered all the three constraints up to optimization to prove that the proposed model is better than the indicator based evolutionary algorithm.

(Emma Fitzgerald *et al.* 2018) discussed about optimal data aggregation and dissemination model in IoT in fog computing environment. This computation storage has multiple sinks than normal single sink model for machine to machine communications. Also actuators are integrated with sensors to measure the data by actual information. Mixed integer programming formulation is used in the proposed model to optimal the routing skills of the network and to reduce the total energy usage per node. Throughput based optimal scheduling is considered in the model to schedule the transmissions and highlights the substantial energy savings which is 13 times greater than the existing model which uses 40 node networks in shortest path flow model.

(Jun Huang *et al.* 2018) proposed an optimization model in M2M communication to improve the QoS in smart cities. An admission control model is proposed in the desired model to obtain the differences in M2M communications and delay sensitive data. The fault tolerance request them into priority queue to access the IoT in the smart cities and a control algorithm is used to improve the QoS in the proposed model which is more effective and feasible in parameters.

(Marian Verhelst and Bert Moons., 2017) discussed about the deep learning neural network based IoT and edge devices applications as a processor technique. Image recognition includes pre-processing, extraction and selection process and this process has computational complexities while obtaining the data so a deep neural network is used until feasible results in power server platforms. Edge devices such as mobiles, IoT nodes, wearble cloths are the trends in present situation. To analyze the data in real time the latency is considered based on the parametric values of the neural networks.

2.4 ROUTING MECHANISM IN MULTIHOP NETWORKS

(Chang *et al.* 2007) discussed about adhoc routing algorithm in proposed model to enhance the throughput of link layer. Transmission rate and interference effects are considered in the theoretical model and a throughput based aware link selection is performed in the proposed model to increase the performance in terms of network throughput. **(Alejandro *et al.* 2008)** proposed an optimal routing algorithm for the wireless Multi-Hop network to enhance the features of the network path. This stochastic routing uses distributed mechanism to create a path from source to destination to transmit data from one network to another network. Figure 2.1 depicts about the classification of multicast routing protocols in MANET based on the applications. Broad classification is performed based on application dependency and independent applications.

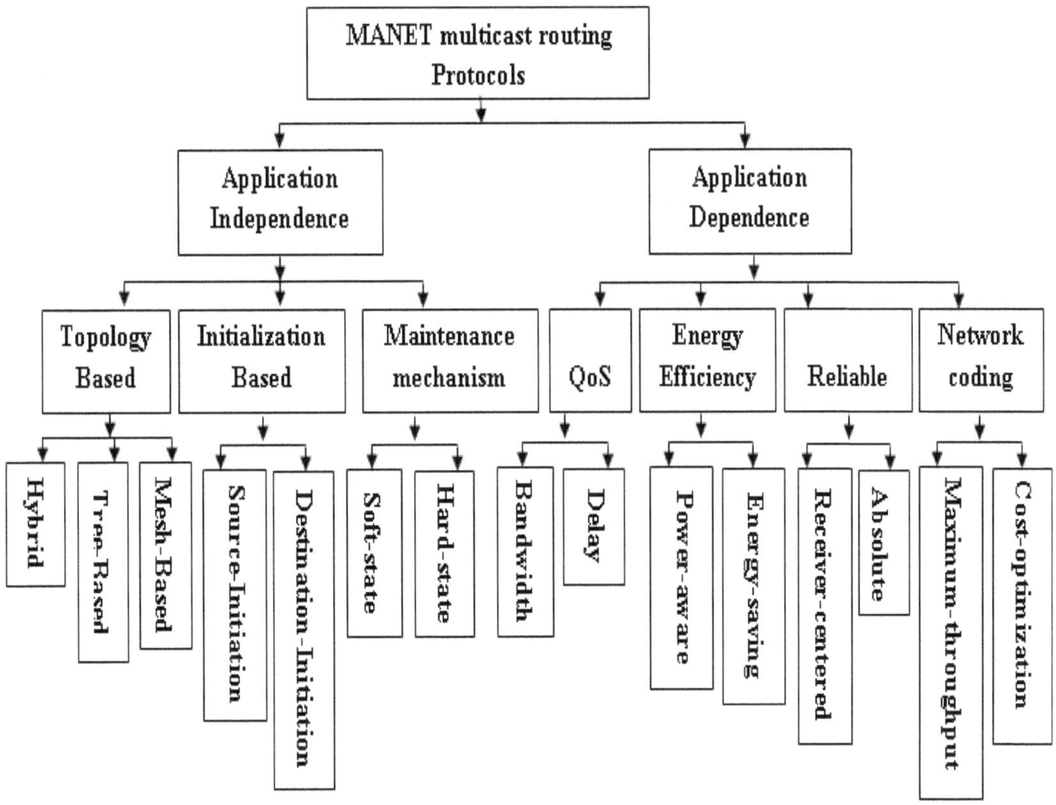

Figure 2.1 Multicast routing Protocols classification based on applications

(Alessandro *et al.* 2009) discussed about a routing algorithm in the multiple vehicle communication which has efficient results in the communication of vehicles. This model minimizes the time between target and its agents based on the proposed strategies and steady state performance of the entire system. The overall performance of the system is obtained at best known of decentralized strategies values. **(Andres *et al.* 2009)** reports about a region based routing mechanism to support NoCs (Network-On-Chip). NoC has many advantages in the networks such as fault tolerance, changing of routing algorithms. Since this advantage consumes much power due to its area, this region based routing mechanism provides efficient mechanism to a network to implement the entries based on the routing table to reduce the power consumption.

(Palesi M Kumar and Catania., 2009) discussed about the Bandwidth-aware routing algorithms available in networks-on-chip (NoC) platforms. The limitation in the NoC depends on the applications and general purpose routing algorithm congested in some cases because of low adaptive nature. To avoid this limitation the proposed model uses high efficient application specific routing algorithms using communication topology and communication bandwidth. The routing adaptive in each router is routed into less traffic links in the application specific routing algorithm for uniform network congestion.

(Cesare *et al.* 2009) proposed an adaptive LLC-Based Hierarchical Power-Aware Routing Algorithm for WSN for successful routing from base station to centre service station. Self-organizing algorithms has energy aware context and this proposed hierarchical based algorithm has solution in terms of scalability, power efficiency and life time. Localized clustering is used in the algorithm to estimate the residual energy present in the nodes to extend the lifetime of the network.

(Chris *et al.* 2011) discusses about Networks-on-Chip dynamic reconfigurable routing in irregular long rang mesh topologies. A standard network algorithm considers the static and dynamic links to avoid the deadlock situation and maintain the connectivity. The proposed routing algorithm has advantage in routing in irregular topologies also based on the runtime LRL insertion and topology reconfiguration. Based on two stage approach this routing relation is defined to calculate the output ports and its applications, calculation of minimal path to prevent dead lock situation.

(Evren Güney *et al.* 2012) reports about the routing problems in WSN and its effective solutions using tabu search heuristic approach in identify the best sensor locations satisfying the coverage requirements. To provide gateway application in WSN most of the applications has efficient management services based on three design issues such as coverage area, data routing and sink location. The proposed model considers these three issues to resolve the routing problems based on this heuristic search approach. Continuous computation tests are carried out to obtain the efficiency and accuracy of the proposed search model.

(Jose Flich *et al.* 2012) discussed various routing algorithms as a survey in research article. Based on the cluster interconnected network topology the routing algorithms are analysed for flexible routing with reduced number of faults. Agnostic routing algorithm is increasingly useful in NoC to find the faults in the 2D mesh topology while the existing models not compatible for NoC operations. **(Manfredi., 2012)** proposed an energy efficient co-operative routing algorithm in WSN. Wireless applications lead in many industrial applications and at the same time it got more attention in the network control system. QoS performance is obtained based on the reliability, efficient of the sensors and amount of energy used. Research aims to reduce this power utilization and to provide better trade off in overall wireless monitoring system. An experimental result compares the proposed model with the minimum power co operative routing algorithm and shortest non cooperative path algorithms in the health care system.

(Arseniy *et.al.*, 2013) discussed about the fault tolerance routing algorithm in NoC using localized detouring paths. In the semiconducting industry the evolution of CMOS enables various features in NoC designs. The interconnections in the NoCs are done through metal wires which affects due to the catastrophic effects. This effect increases the faults in system and it needs routing algorithms for fault tolerance to maintain the connectivity inside the NoC. The proposed model uses this fault tolerance algorithm to handle the dead lock situation.

(Auon Muhammad Akhtar *et al.* 2013) reports about usage of co-operative physical layer efficient energy routing in a network using physical layer network coding scheme. The proposed model used two routing algorithm to implement the co operative layer network coding (CPLNC) with high energy gain upto 62% when compared to conventional shortest path algorithms. Incorporating the energy efficient routing algorithm and threshold distance the CPLNC uses point to point transmission to reduce the energy consumption. **(Baoxian *et al.* 2014)** proposed a bidirectional routing algorithm for multi constrained situations. This bidirectional search has effective strategy in route acquisition and identifies the shortest path considering the nodes. K shortest path is used in bidirectional search to reduce the complexity, also it is used to converge the QoS routing algorithm. Bidirectional multi constrained routing algorithm is used to support the IP networks.

(Lapas Praditasnee *et al.* 2014) proposed an efficient route update and maintenance protocol in large scale sensor networks. A continuous change in the channel affects the performance of the network and also this literature highlights the global and local process in route updating process using hierarchical routing framework. DSDV, DSPV with Ipv6 protocol is compared in terms of reception ratio in the proposed model for low power WSN network.

2.5 OTHER ROUTING MECHANISMS

In IoT and multihoming other than the routing protocols which is discussed earlier some more detailed research articles also studied to obtain keen knowledge about routing protocols. This section provides a simple description about such routing protocols.

2.5.1 Data routing:

(Ali Rıza *et al.* 2016) proposed an allocation model in a heterogeneous network based on the user allocation and data rate allocation. Mobile terminal and wireless access points are considered in the proposed model for offering bandwidth to the applications with high data rates. This proposed model uses mixed integer nonlinear program to represent the computational complexity in the network. This problem is resolved by convex optimization model and this heuristic algorithm reduces the computational complexity in the heterogeneous wireless networks.

2.5.2 Green routing:

(Bruno *et al.* 2017) discussed about the central based low power lossy system using green routing. This proposed model uses centrality based green routing protocol to improve the network performance and reduce the power consumption. Green routing is a collection of tree protocols and it chooses nodes for data fusion and link quality estimation to obtain the routes, energy efficiency, consumption in the WSN. Finally a policy aware algorithm is used in the proposed algorithm to balance the energy consumption.

2.5.3 Geographic routing;

(Haojun Huang *et al.* 2017) discusses about geographic routing in WSN to send multiple messages from source to destination to conserve the resources using energy efficient multicast routing. This methodology utilizes the information about the nodes based on the location instead of information about the nodes. This efficient routing resolves the challenges present in the WSN employing energy aware multicast tree and a set of destination and source nodes. Basic metrics used in message delivery adaptively selects the nearby optimal nodes and forwards the conservations. An experimental result shows that proposed model achieves performance in parameters such as energy consumption, control overhead and computational complexity.

2.5.4 Software Defined Routing

(Manisekaran S.V and Venkatesan R., 2016) discusses about software defined routing algorithm for WSN. The proposed model considers the energy consumption and bandwidth utilization as factors in calculating the life time of the network. Software Defined Network (SDN) allocates separate channels in data plane and control plane to increase the speed of the network and also it maintains the battery usage based on the indispensible parameters such as throughput, energy consumption and delay latency.

2.6 FINDINGS OF THE SURVEY

An elaborate survey of research contributions has been done in this literature survey chapter to introduce the multihoming concepts in various wireless sensor networks. It has been elaborately described on basis of various literature work under the categories multihoming, multi path, multi casting. Internet of things has been discussed in detail for implementing IoT in multi homing environment. From the research ideas the concept of integrating IoT into Multihoming provides better solution in a multipath communication by reducing the complexity and increasing the efficiency in terms of energy, power allocation and routing mechanisms. Many optimization models are discussed in the IoT for better results and third phase of the survey consists of routing model details in WSN. In the era of Wireless Sensor Networks routing algorithm plays a vital role and in the same manner in multihoming also various routing algorithms are analysed. Adhoc Routing, Region Based Routing, Hierarchical Power-Aware Routing Algorithm, application specific routing, green routing, Software Defined Routing which are discussed in various research works are summarized based on the common issues present in the model. From this research survey the next chapter describes about the general multihoming concepts and integration of internet of things (IoT) with multi homing through routing algorithms are discussed.

CHAPTER 3

MULTI HOMING IoT

Internet of things has wide range of applications in many areas includes smart management systems and multi path connectivity management such as automatic air interface, optimal load balancing in network traffics in the cloud environment and others network applications. This reliable mechanism in the multihoming industry produces a system that consists of increased mobility and bandwidth requirements which are essential factor in the networking. This chapter deals with the introduction about the multi homing IoT and its classifications.

3.1 INTRODUCTION

Multi homing networks has exponential growth in its field due to the availability of devices and communication technologies. This paradigm has wide access to increase the resilience, dependability and entire network performance in the server side. In the present scenario the manufactures from the spectrum node have implemented the various integrated technologies in order to access the network via this multi path or multi band methods. Multiple access technologies are implemented in the heterogeneous networks based on the static policies of user inputs and its corresponding outputs. In the view of utilizing the ubiquitous communication the network must have the capability to connect different networks and its resources. Also it must lead to the innovative applications to meet out the goals in the present updating network. This multihoming concept uses various transport protocols to deal the active path failure and its correction methods in a multi path environment. This mechanism also has multi access and multi homing model in the active path to prevent the network deployment.

3.2 MULTIHOMING IN IOT

Generally multi homing is integrated into concepts such as multiple addressing, interfaces, overlay routing in the networks. Considering an example that multiple addresses is assigned to connect different terminals if the given network has prefixes on each connection then there may be a problem of overlapping in the address terminals. Since the multiple address has more similarities in the variables and less similarities in their variations. This over lapping concept in the network must be reconfigured over the entire network coverage area to sustain the user connectivity in the network. Overlay routing is basically integrated into a inter domain routing mechanism to increase the fault tolerance level of the model. This multi homing concept is simply classified into three categories such as

1. End- Host Multi Homing
2. End- Site Multi Homing
3. Hybrid Multi Homing

Along with the multi homing concept internet of things is also integrated to introduce a new applications. This internet of things (IoT) was first proposed by Kevin Ashton in 1999 by referring the interconnected objects in the radio frequency technology environment. Based on the applications the definition of internet of things (IoT) has many visions to provide solution for the many internet business groups for connecting many things into a single network. The definition for internet of things is given by European Research Cluster (ERC) as

"If a system has self configuring capabilities based on the communication standards and its protocols in terms of physical or virtual for the dynamic global infrastructure network, then the things which are identical in the physical attributes and intelligent interference are integrated into a single informative network as Internet of Things (IoT) "

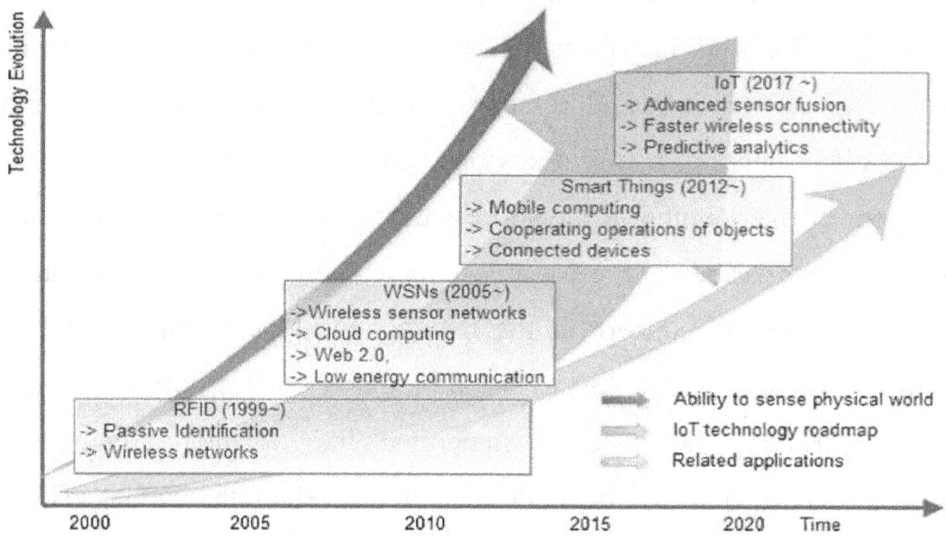

Figure 3.1 Growth of Internet of Things in present century

The growth of internet of things and its related researches are highlighted in the figure 3.1. It starts from year 2000 and ends in 2020 proposes the IoT applications has wide range in the future trends to enhance the advanced sensor fusion researches to improve the wireless connectivity. Figure 3.2 depicts an illustration of enterprise multi homing model and also includes ISP and Enterprise network which are interconnected through the links of internets.

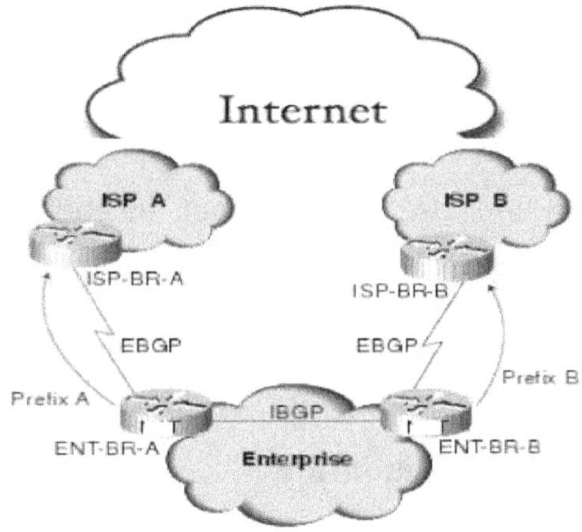

Figure 3.2 Illustration of Enterprise Multi Homing

3.2.1 End-host Multihoming

End host Multihoming is an entity configuration which includes several hop connection to the terminal end to select its own connection. Different logical or physical interfaces are used in the multihomed hose to interface the various networks and each network is configured by the service model. Prefix 1 and prefix 2 are the two interfaces used in the physical interface connections and it can be extended up to "n" numbers.

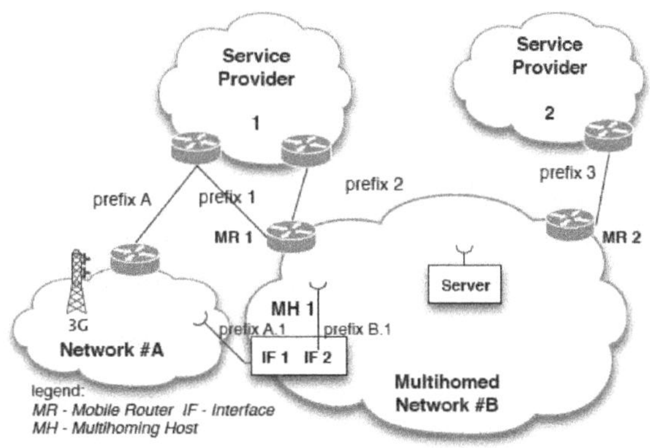

Figure 3.3 End Host Illustration- Multihoming Host

This multiple prefixes are used to configure the links and to access the network routers. Figure 3.3 is a descriptive picture about Multihoming Host environment. From the figure it is observed that two service providers are used to connect in the main network which uses connecting lines as prefix1, 2,3 for service provider 1 and 2. For network A, Prefix A is used as a connecting line to join in a multihomed network.

3.2.2 End-site Multihoming

In the network configurations the first hop connections are given to the destinations to define the end site multihoming model. Based on the definitions for the end site multihoming multiple connections are used in the internet to increase the reliability of the network and also to improve the entire performance. This end site multi homing has redundant network connections which allows many networks for its services. The home agent and mobile routers are considered in the end site multihoming to provide internet access for the users in the network.

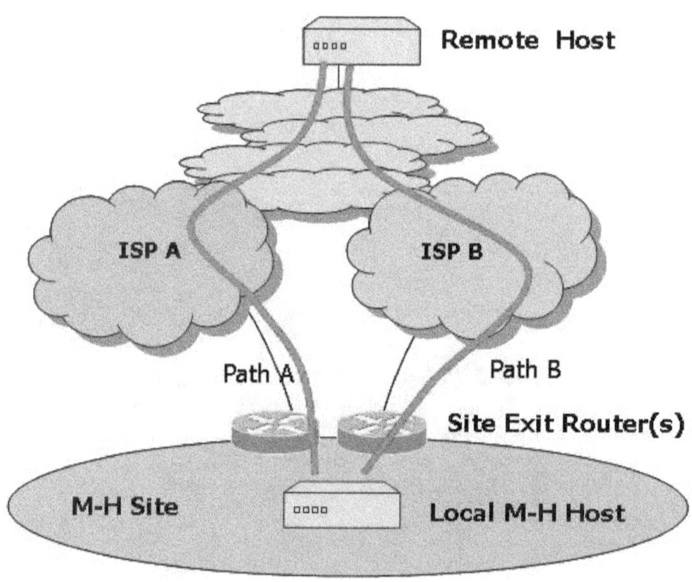

Figure 3.4 Illustration of End site modelling

End site multihoming model process is simply based on the configuration and its problem orientation has various parameters such as home agents, number of available prefixes and allocation of address in the internet service provided model. Figure 3.4 shows an illustration about the End site hosting model.

3.3 VISION OF THE INTERNET OF THINGS

The vision of internet of things is used to develop a real and virtual environment in order to create a smart energy, cities and many intelligent applications. IoT has enormous amount of envision in the real time scenario and is ideally used to connect anyone at anywhere at any condition. The direct definition for internet of things given by ERC makes this into a much more advanced model than other technologies such as M2M connections, RFID and 4G communication. Future storage services are highly distributed and people starts to use smart objects in various platforms. Since the wired and wireless applications all belongs to the internet resources all decentralized networks must be interconnected in the future to resolve the consumer needs. Convergence of customers, industrial internet users makes an effective opening for the field of IoT in order to handle the peoples in the network, data and other cloud oriented things. This cloud to IoT connect things generally transmits large data to create a service which has no issues in the connectivity and intelligence. The future vision of Internet of Things depends on various factors and in content aware computing, Seamless Connectivity and Interoperability, Network neutrality is mainly considered to provide a best network to the user for their needs.

Context aware computing is a popular term in the IoT since optimization is necessary to enhance the performance of the network. The non-interactive behaviour in the multi user heterogeneous environment has significant challenges in the business applications which acquire and analyze the relevant information from the user. Based on the data collected from the user this computing technique has ability to select the suitable service to the user needs based on the current situation with minimum interactions. Seamless connectivity and interoperability deals with the syntactical interface and software architectures in the communication infrastructure to integrate the computational artefacts such as hardware and software. It mainly shares the information between the heterogeneous devices in the large scale networks.

Network neutrality is another factor in the IoT vision which has power efficient devices for communicating interconnected devices. By providing a most appropriate connectivity to user on all the times from any path based on the principles of internet service providers is a key factor in the network neutrality. In an emergency situations, In order to treat all the users in a common way even when the network is over loaded, This network neutrality puts an effort in the environment for uninterrupted service. If this neutral service is not available in the network then user may be affected and forced to move into locked situation and this creates problems to the users and also to the service providers. To avoid this kind of risk issues a mutual agreement has been established in many organizations with other service providers to hold the users and also to maintain the service.

3.4 APPLICATIONS OF THE INTERNET OF THINGS

Internet of Things (IoT) has a wide range of applications and in this research topic it is mainly classified into categories such as

- Smart City
- Smart Energy
- Smart Health

- Smart Infrastructures
- Smart Transport

Based on these categories various applications are available in the present scenario and it is limited up to this small list. Based on the research works over few years these applications are listed out under the IoT domain.

Under smart city categories big data analysis are performed to describe the applications in IoT. Smart parking system is a simple example that provides details about the spaces available in the parking lot. Smart infrastructure deals with the structural health of the buildings and other construction sites which provides details about the strength and material conditions.

Smart transportation is an another application that provides details about the real time transportation details in the urban areas, vehicle monitoring, optimization of routes to the users. Maps are another application in the smart transportation which provides interactive system to the users in driving conditions. An intelligent highway has real time warnings about the traffic and unexpected events is another application under this smart transportation.

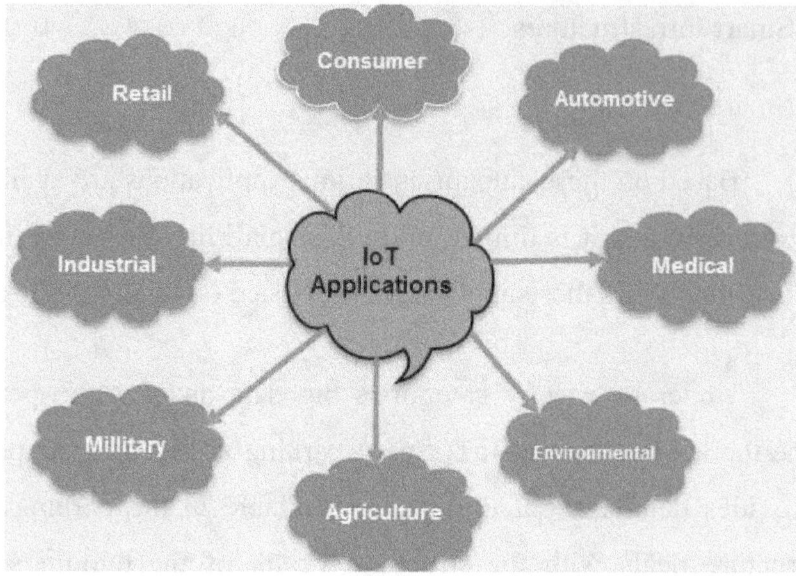

Figure 3.5 IoT applications

Smart resource management Zdeals with the applications such as forest fire detection, air pollution, earth quake detection, water management systems. The level of combustion gases and alert zones are useful to the users to get aware about the fire. Smart air pollution monitoring system monitors the level of toxic or unwanted gases emitted from the industries. Various landslides are predicted earlier using this smart application and the land conditions and its patters are observed through this kind of applications. Earth quake detection and water quality in rivers and sea is another kind of applications in the smart energy management. Detection of water leakages and water pressure data leads to tremendous researches in many applications while in searching the irrigation systems. Smart management deals with water and environment management which deals with the utilization data of resources in a summarized view and that can be useful for analyzing the data for the future use.

Smart Grid and Smart metering deal with applications such as tank level monitoring in the oil and gas corporation cisterns, while the smart grid manage and provides essential data about the energy consumption. Solar energy management monitoring the performance of photovoltaic cells is essential and this smart grid system becomes solution to this application. Smart retail and logistics deals the supply chain control for monitoring the traceability of goods. An intelligent shopping application has details about the sales value, customer preference data and products details along with their validity dates. This helps to maintain a data base for the entire products and analysis provides a clear view to the users.

A smart industrial control application deals with the M2M applications for diagnosis and controls. Temperature monitoring, Ozone Presence monitoring are the weather oriented smart applications that deal the weather data and its effects due to the industrial exploitation. A Zigbee, UWB, RFID based smart applications are available in the indoor location for smart real time communications. Apart from this agricultural and farming also includes this smart management system which acquires the green house facts, enhancing the food processing, furthermore many real time applications are available using Internet of Things.

3.5 MULTIHOMING AND TRANSPORT PROTOCOLS

Multihoming transport protocols and its standards by IETF is considered in the applications of IoT for data transfer and other process. TCP is used as multi homing option for connection establishment based on the present position and primary path. If the essential path has been established then the address inclusion or deletion process can be availed by the user for conveying the information from source to destination. In the multi homing reception all the paths are created for certain amount of time even for the unregistered users. TCP supports Multihoming by focusing the resiliency path failures and the availability of interfaces. It doesn’t enable the bandwidth sharing along various paths and it only employs multiple TCPs for all available paths to provide independency. TCP fairness is an application that is used to create parallel connections for utilizing the network resources and also this TCP manages the master congestion control in the network to obtain the overall sending rate and its sub flows.

An extension of TCP is developed to enhance the multihoming features in terms of end to end throughput. Based on the different functionalities a sender and a receiver have selective acknowledgments in this process and also an estimated round trip time is calculated for each process in the starting itself. This control mechanism has track records of data types and bandwidth conditions and delay timings. The limitation in the fast TCP is throughput, since it has less value during the network congestion situations, One way measurement is established to overcome the limitation of fast TCP for avoiding the round trip time estimates.

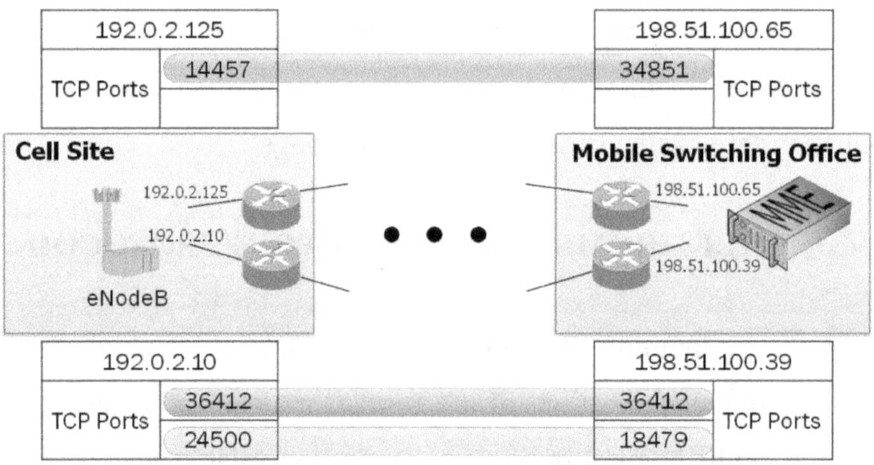

Figure 3.6 TCP in Multihoming

An illustration of multi homing transport layer TCP is depicted in figure 3.6 which includes the TCP ports, mobile switching office and cell site for the source to destination communication through IP address. TCP using multiple network interfaces has simultaneous connections in the heterogeneous interfaces to modify the TCP connection. A standard transport protocol and this modified TCP differentiate themselves in path allocation and also in resource management. Another TCP is employed in certain network which used primary back up model to reach the particular address to support the multi priority flow on the master management process. TCP layer is essential in the multihoming applications for data transfer and other data oriented applications.

3.6 MULTIHOMING AND MOBILITY MANAGEMENT

MultiHoming transport management mainly depends on the TCP while the TCP includes the internet protocols based on various versions such as IPv6, Ipv4 protocols. The future support of multi homing is available on the IPv6 since IPv4 doesn't support the features present in it. IPv6 has large degree of operational freedom due to its degree and mobility management compared to IPv4. Even though it has advantages over IPv4 it has limitations in terms of mobility management, Since the established communication is considered to maintain connection across the network the IPv6 doesn't have enough support for this process. If there is a change in the IP home address than IPv6 does not support for the new address and it doesn't have enough survivability.

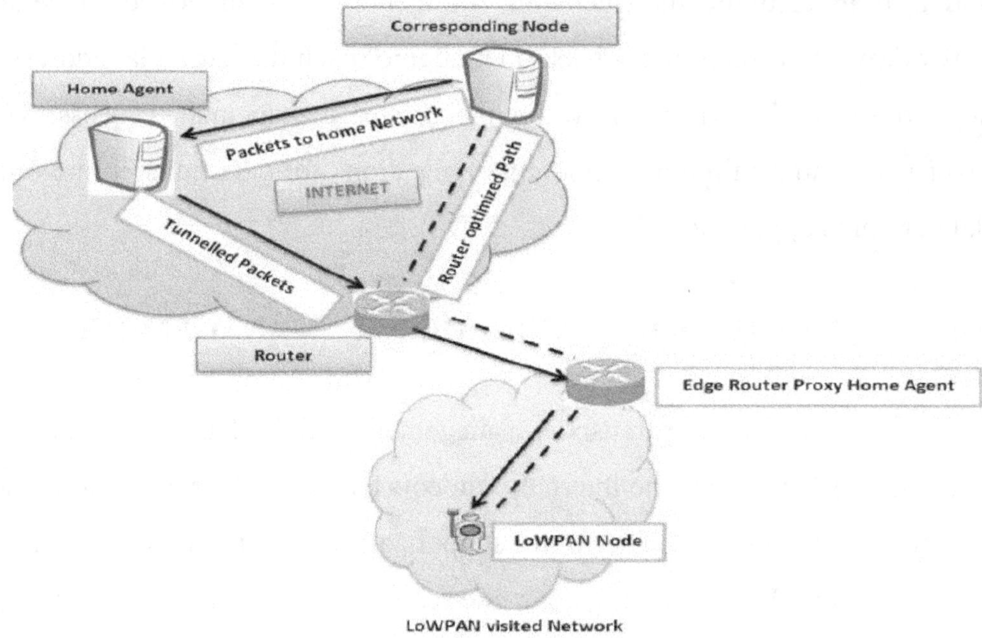

Figure 3.7 IPv6 Overview

Proxy mobile IPv6 is another network management protocol which has network mobility management to overcome the issues in IPv6. Mainly it introduces local mobility anchor and mobile access gateway. In this, mobility anchor acts as mobile node and mobile gateway access has router management options. It supports the address in prefix and suffixes. The most efficient configuration for simultaneous connection shares IP address and it has limitations in terms of multi link subnet issue. For each process the proxy version 6 provides separate path but the subnet has same value for the entire connections makes the IPv6 version into a limitation. The PMIPv6 supports all the limitations present in v6 and successive models. It has unique address on each interfaces and a dedicated prefix suffix is included for providing a unique address across the interface.

Multiple address and flow bindings allows MIPv6 to handle the multiple address issues. Several address and for each mobile node a permanent address is employed as a binding unique identification number.

All this process are informed by a single message containing all the information from source to destination along with the link characteristics. The specification of flow binding has specifications in multihoming context exchange. A particular address and specification policies are mapped to user preference due to its specificity.

3.7 HYBRID MULTIHOMING

Hybrid multihoming broadly classified into three categories such as Content centric approach, Locator identifier split approach, Routing centric approach. In this the Content centric approach is used to perform routing based on the node and its interest in the network to exchange information. The architecture for service integration for supporting multihoming is added advantage in the content centric approach. In case of optimizing the future internet it incorporates the cross layer schemes for various functionalities. Service centric end to end abstraction approach has transfer of data from one node to nearest node to support flow distribution. Network named content mainly focuses on the data operations. If the node is interested in sending packet types and NNC codes then based on the distinct table values the interest packets are transferred from one node to another node. These packets carry only about the information and not about the location. This hierarchical structure supports mobility and flowdistribution.

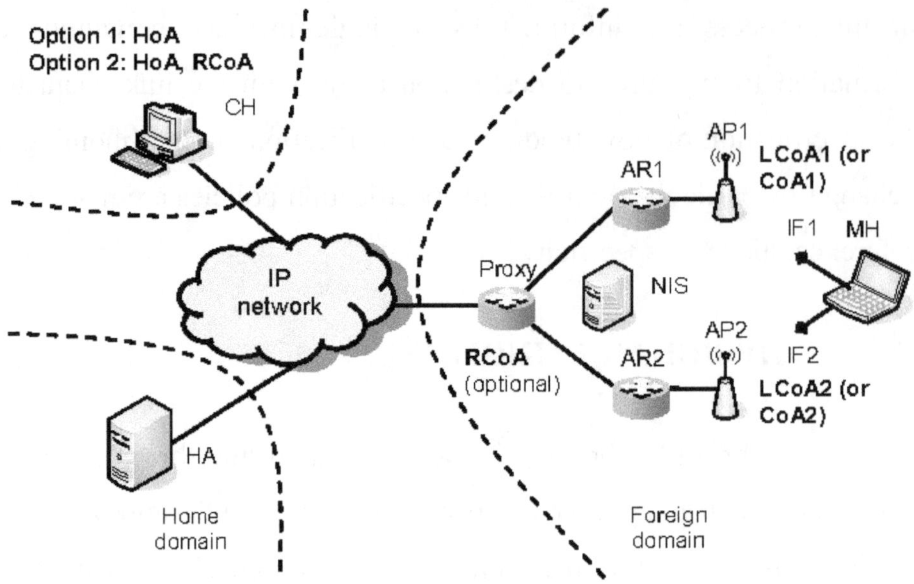

Figure 3.8 Hybrid Multihoming Model

Data oriented network architecture is used to generate key mechanism in the routing based client server process. This method has reply for each client for finding the packets and the transport layer binds each name in the header and not the IP address in the TCP layer. This model assures the shortest path communication based on the confirmation from the server data and supports multiple connections since it has no public codes. Multiple access information models allow information creation, distribution and retrieval among various nodes in the networks. It supports the local and global domain resources for name resolution services. This service has details about the applications and its domains and not about the details on information. Mobility and multihoming support is an advantage in the multiple access information system in the present internet world and a real time example is an implementation in Firefox and thunderbird browsers.

3.8 SUMMARY

This chapter describes about a brief description about multi homing and its associated research areas along with internet of things (IoT).

Various network models and its types are analyzed in the first portion of chapter includes End- Host Multi Homing, End- Site Multi Homing, Hybrid Multi Homing. End host and end site multi homing models are analyzed based on the advantages and its limitations. Hybrid multi homing is discussed based on the content centric approach which provides a suitable mechanism to the multihoming environment. While considering multihoming mobility management and the research based results MIPv6 is suitable in the transport applications of multihoming along with this hybrid model.

CHAPTER 4

ETSI-M2M BASED IDENTIFICATION SCHEMES IN HETEROGENEOUS IOT NETWORKS

Internet plays a vital role in global communication and it has set of standard protocols to connect various wireless and wired devices to form a heterogeneous networks and related applications in academics, governments, business etc. Earlier version of internet usage is limited into specific task such as mails and websites for information sharing. In present scenario internet is essential in all the applications due to the digital era. Starting from simple life styles to major organization oriented applications this internet provides plenty of services to meet out the individual needs and also organization needs. The secret behind this internet oriented applications is due to the user friendly automated systems and the utilization of digitalization technologies. Demand of using this internet oriented task leads to many research in all aspects since it becomes a mandatory in user's life and this count increases day by day. The increased connectivity based applications provides simple solution to the complex applications and also creates many issues and challenges. Internet of things is one of the leading researches that provide promising solutions to the many data handling and processing applications. IoT provides a better frame work to allow user to interact to virtual world in real time which allows user to look up for the information for what they really needs in the daily life. This chapter discusses about the presence of IoT in a heterogeneous network based on the ETSI M2M based architecture. The summary of identification schemes and formats are evaluated based on the present research issues and a solution is provided for the simple management problem. Finally this chapter evaluates the performance of the proposed model using the identifier model and calculates the parameters based on the Energy consumption, data payload, Mobility cost and signaling cost.

4.1 INTRODUCTION

In today's world common services use internet to interact the applications and the task to identify its extent is simply given as Internet of Things to ensure that endpoint things are independent to the user needs. Since the applications depend on internet, user identification process is essential to explain the user identity and also it lead to the system into a secure system. Such identification model provides easy access to end users to keep their information safe by enabling a safety procedure. In general identification model has issues in its security as any user can obtain the other personal informations using this enabled service in a heterogeneous network. IoT has simple explanation for this attributes based on the identifier module and a common attribute based identify module available in market is Radio frequency identifier tag. This has real meaning and it differentiates the other objects depends on the various concepts. Identifier uses a unique way to serve strong identification system for single purpose use and it also enables the sharing based entities to resolve the issues. Designing such identifier and its solutions based on the application provide an added advantage to the users and it is considered as a benefit in the IoT based heterogeneous environment.

4.2 HETEROGENEOUS IOT NETWORKS

Generally heterogeneous networks consists of various application oriented devices and if it discusses in terms of IoT based heterogeneous network then this system is considered as a better eco system for smart applications which is very much helpful in improving the system performance and also the user satisfaction. IoT is defined based on the statement that everything should be connected for improving the user standards in daily activities. IoT and M2M are inter-related technology that provides support and connectivity for the users. IoT consists of many sensors and actuators to connect the network and hence uses wireless sensor networks. IoT gateway is integrated into IoT applications to connect various sensors such as Bluetooth, 802.11a/b and Zigbee for transmission of data to the IoT cloud. Gateway uses multiple interfaces to support all the available technologies present in the network as a connectivity model in the wired and wireless systems. The presence of IoT gateway has interfaces to provide connectivity to the internet to realize the utilization factor of the entire network. A cost based specific solution is essential in wireless sensor networks and IoT provides the solution. IoT gateway provides individual connectivity to the users to provide better connectivity by generating standard service gateway.

The difference in normal gateway and the service gateway is mainly based on the amount of data generated in the WSN heterogeneous network. It provides better connectivity to the users by connecting internet through this gateway and it has very few numbers of interfaces. Service gateway has subset of technologies depending on the IoT and its proximity based services. Figure 4.1 provides an illustration of gateway representation in the wireless environment which consists of various cells such as macro cell, micro cell and Pico cell in the mobile communication environment. It has direct backhaul link to establish connection between the users and the main service provider. Second relay cell is used to enhance the services in extended or isolated areas. Finally fiber is used to connect the service gateway and the components present in the entire network

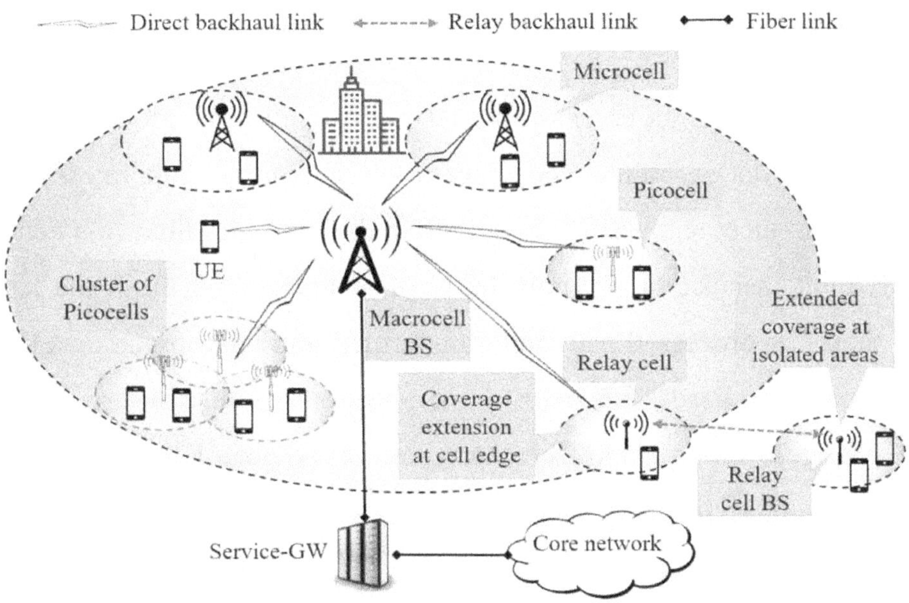

Figure 4.1 illustration of routing model in IoT using service gateway module.

Gateway used WSN has capacity to convert information from one form to other using the recent supported environment. Conventional gateway and the secure IoT based gateway supports in processing large data. Generally the path of gateway comprised a huge amount of data and this is essential in future analysis to lead the IoT network in the WSN. Millions of IoT has multiple gateways to provide a generic path to reduced throughput. The usage of multi homing has interfaces to provide a secure data path orientation. The proposed wireless model uses parallel data analyzing model. By encouraging a band frequency allocation is performed which is used as model using gateway. Secures standard gateway model simply follows and leads to congestion. The routing technique is discussed to develop routing techniques by varying load conditions.

4.3 WIRELESS SENSOR NETWORKS

WSN is an essential model in designing IoT model; it uses data from sensor nodes, collect and process the data and collaborates with other nodes to connect end users through internal or external link. In a centralized WSN cloud service has responsibility of acquiring data from the terminals and then it is processed and then transformed into appropriate data based on the application need. This helps the application to sense and react based on the changes in the data from terminal to device. Figure 4.2 gives an illustration of heterogeneous sensor network in WSN and it contains sensors to collect the information and a sink or base station is used to send the collected data to the external network.

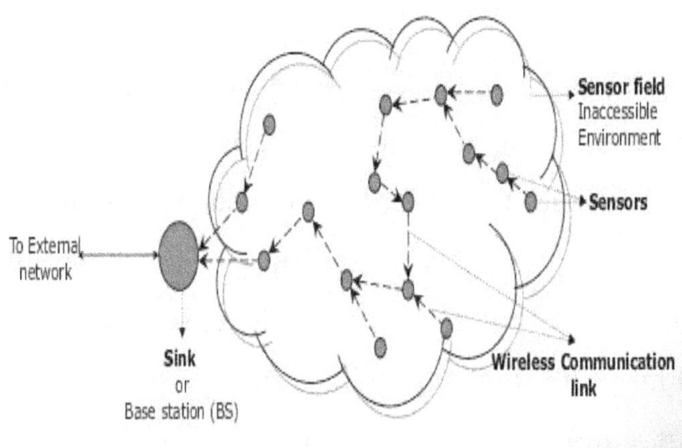

Figure 4.2 illustration of WSN IoT

In the distributed network the raw data accessed from the sensors is pre-processed using high level intelligent devices. This dynamic collaboration differentiates the applications from the common WSN platform. The two types of IoT in WSN provide benefits in identifying the user needs and secure authentication communication from device to terminal. Based on the multiple entities IoT applications use sensing nodes, service providers and authenticated processing systems which turns out the entire model into a secure communication model as per the common user need.

4.4 IDENTIFICATION SCHEMES IN IOT

The identification schemes are essential in IoT since there are various identification modules are available based on the application which is limited based on human ingenuity, industrial standards and specifications. A summary of various identification schemes are discussed here to resolve the issues based on the limitations in the system design.

RFID object identifiers use an established code for structuring the communication module that can be used to accommodate the legal standards that differs from GS1. The limitation that is present in the model is lack for resolver address if it is different from OID structures apart from this limitation this identifier does not have any marketing budgets as per the ISO standards due to its centralized nature.

Global Electronic product code has the advantages in terms of design which is developed based on the GS1 bar code standards and the utilization covers major areas based on the applications by retailers due to the end to end code architecture. The limitation in this identifier module is due to limited uncertain RFID data options, cost of source in marketing to the retailers and privacy issues on post sales.

Short OID has advantages similar to RFID approach so that the requirements meet the entire OID standards and all the applications need an encoding scheme to provide a secure communication. The limitation present in the module is it lags in performance while resolving the address that is present in OID structure. The main issue in this is it lags in domain specific applications since it cannot make differentiations from the users and terminals.

NFC has major advantage due to its significant infrastructure and it provides an added advantage as an individual ownership to all users due to its investment in individual design. The limitation in this model is discussed based on its air specific protocol and low data capture integration. Moreover its similarity to 2D bar codes is found as another limitation in the model.

OID is an established system model for e-products in the domain with increased numbers within the network. Based on the product expenditure the application increases and this becomes an issue that it needs additional infrastructure to compensate the additional application design. Another limitation of this model is it is not suitable for physical layer applications since it does not have any data carriers.

Ubiquitous code is an established code in Japan that resolves the process through TRON engine which has potential to process parallel computing systems. The limitation in the design is due to the reverse logic used in the data transfer process and it is not much powerful as global EPC.

URL is an identifier used in WSN which uses an established system to support alias short form of URL. It has limitation in terms of URL length since the URL does not allow the users for long length data capture and it contains security issues in it.

IP address as an identifier has advantages since it enables the M2M communication which is suitable for long term communication and monitoring process. It is applicable for most of the IoT applications. It has some limitation due to its light weight objects and resource constrains and scalability problems.

4.5 ETSI M2M ARCHITECTURE

The ETSI M2M architecture is used as reference architecture in communication which is adopted by main European telecommunication standards based on set of standards in middle ware communications. It defines the entities and functions for deployment of interoperable IoT application which underlies the network technologies for providing efficient delivery services. Transparency and interoperability are the common resources used in the IoT application as building blocks which claim the development and also the deployment of the module. The main system architecture is based on the present network and the user application standards and once all the factors are defined then a service layers on network domain is pre-planned based on the M2M device and its standards. The functions are shared by the entities present in the M2M reference points for communication management, application management, device discovery and management, security and data processing. Based on the ETSI technical standards the architecture of ETSI M2M is defined and the key entities used in M2M are defined in terms of M2M device, M2M GW, M2M applications, M2M area network and M2M network applications. Figure 4.3 shows a high level ETSI M2M architecture defined by the ETSI technical standards.

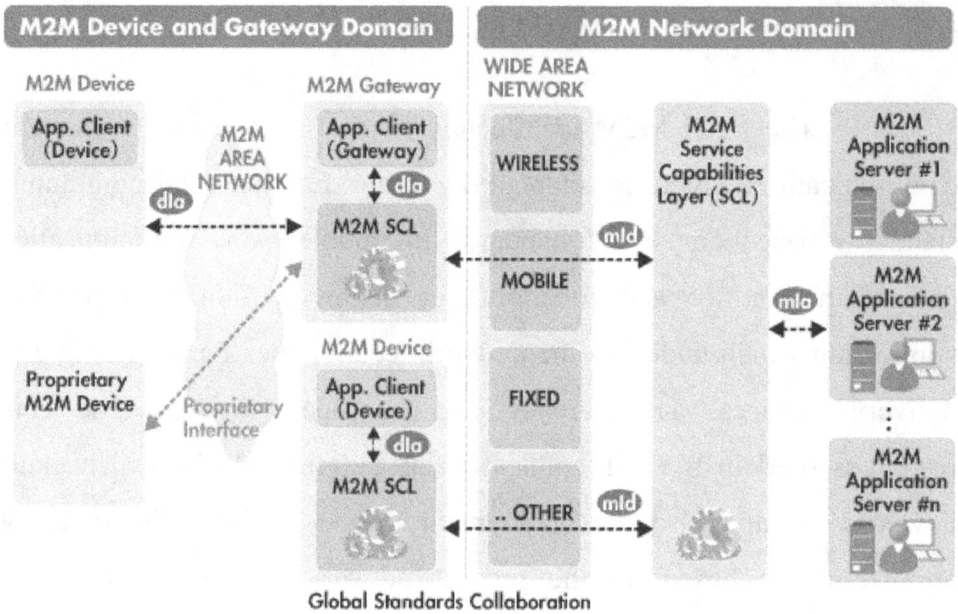

Figure 4.3 ETSI- M2M Architecture

- **M2M DEVICE** runs based on the applications using network domain functions.
- **M2M GW** provides a guarantee service to M2M devices for interconnection of network and its interoperability factors.
- **M2M APPLICATIONS** are used to run the service logic and service capabilities through some reference point in the application.
- **M2M NETWORK** used domain based connectivity between the GW and M2M applications.
- **M2M NETWORK APPLICATIONS** uses application domain to run the service logic and it has capabilities to access the interfaces.
- **M2M AREA NETWORK** provides connections between the device and GW.

The network and application specific domain is used to access the network through the transport layer and M2M core. The connectivity between the device domain and core network depends on the application domain. Universal mobile telecommunication systems, WLAN, UWB, WiMaX are used as an access technologies in the M2M applications. This core networks has network applications to provide IP connectivity and interconnections. The network SCL is used to manage the data processing and access control process while routing process takes places since it acts as a communication model based on the M2M capabilities. Applications that can control and send commands to M2M GW are based on the device domain which is formed by the standards of M2M and it can connect directly to the application domain for accessing the network. Figure 4.4 describes the M2M communication model starting from device, gateway domain. M2M network domain is used for connection establishment process.

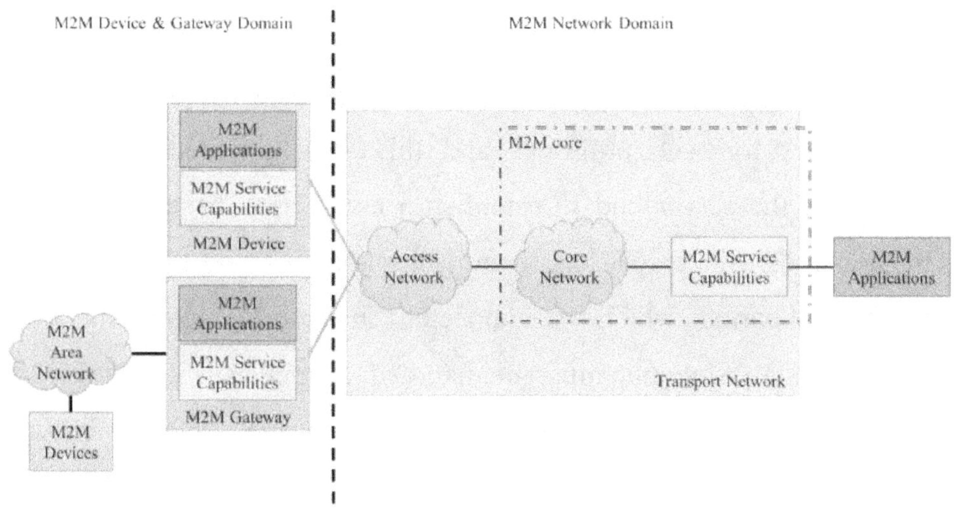

Figure 4.4 Illustration of M2M communication module

In case if the device runs on M2M applications then it must have M2M SCL standards to access the network for the M2M devices. Due to limitation in this process M2M devices provide services only to the M2M applications and it is not comparing with the ETSI Standards. Devices with legacy issues have limitation if it does not use the standard interface they can't be able to connect in the M2M application system so that it needs a M2M GE to obtain a temporary proxies so that the connections is possible. M2M GW run software components based on the SCL and GW applications and it requires sensors and devices which are connected through a gate way domain for allowing the legacy devices to connect SCL.

The area network provides connectivity between the inbuilt devices and for specific applications it needs some reference measures to allow other devices to communicate with the inbuilt applications. This reference point allows others to communicate in the network domain and then access is provided through GW on the network domain. Figure 4.5 provides a proposed ETSI based system architecture in IoT domain application in multihoming. It has clients which uses internet as a common entity since all the applications used on the internet.

The server portion in the middle part of the proposed model uses HTTP servers for web programs and this TCP oriented operations are controlled in the server end to establish a connection based on M2M and ETSI standards. Since IoT has in built applications and also other sensor oriented application which is connected in heterogeneous manner the connection establishments must be handled as per the standards. In the terminal end sensor mode network is connected through gateway for various terminals. The devices communicate with other networks through the server model and the clients are interconnected for updates of data from the sensor network. IP based gateway is used in the proposed model for handling the standard issues in the ETSI architecture.

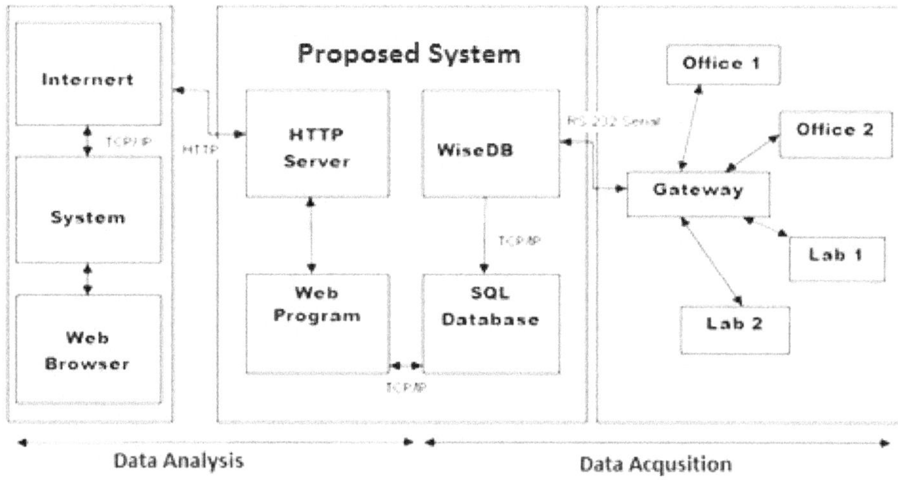

Figure 4.5 Proposed Multi-Homing Model based on ETSI-M2M model

M2M management functions all the requirements to manage applications on M2M SC in network domain for managing the access core, transport networks. The proposed model has management functions as performance management, fault management, firmware management, configuration management and all the management functions includes installing and upgrading the applications in M2M domain.

4.6 IDENTIFIER FORMATS

The identifier formats are essential in the communication since all the process are related to the information's provided by the user device are verified based on this formats. So that the interface becomes easy in user domain and also in network domain for build in devices and also for legacy devices. The proposed identifier model is suitable in IoT domain applications. Figure 4.6 provides description about the identifier format used in network domain. It consists of frame control bits, sequence numbers, address fields, frame identifiers code, configuring payload, and frame check sequence. The frame control is a 2 octet bits which control the frame process and the sequence number provides information about the order of the frame when multiple frames send to the server at a common time.

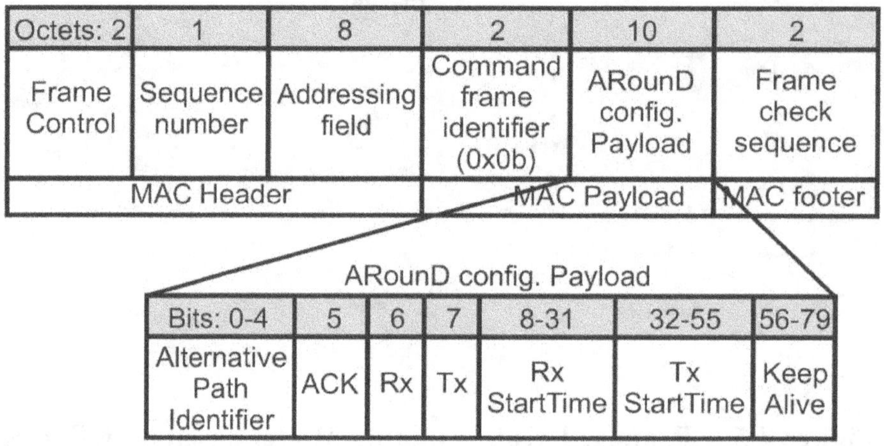

Figure 4.6 Identifier Format used in domain

Address field refers that destination point and also about the source point for efficient transmission without any miss interruption. Configure payload bits is used to configure the frame to the destination point address so that this helps to create configurations like acknowledgement, receiver point, transmitter point and the status of the process including starting time and end time of transmission and reception. For fundamental identification of system a combination of identifiers is combined in the proposed model and the format is given as

----

||||| |

Frame check sequence is used to check the foot sequence in the MAC. Things in Multihoming IoT is represented into identifier and based on the identifier format different attributes are related as follows

The proposed identifier format has advantages over lifetime, scalability, performance such as end to end delay, reduced energy and increased through put. The main aim of this identifier format is to serve automatic identification and connection establishment in the network in the complicated integration of software components and user preference based on the universal standards.

4.7 RESULTS AND DISCUSSION

The Proposed model is implemented based on the identifier format and parameters like signalling cost and mobility related cost are evaluated based on the experimentations conducted in MatLab 14.1 on a system with configuration of Intel i7 Processor with 2.5 GHz frequency using 4GB as memory. The evaluation performance of the proposed compares the architecture based on the sensor nodes and number of hops. Finally the performance comparison is done with Romain *et al.* and Huang *et al.* model. Table 4.1 provides the details of parameters used in the experimentation in proposed model.

Table 4.1 Specification of Simulation Parameters

S.No	Parameters	Value
1	No of WSN Node	50
2	Node density	0.0017-0.0082
3	Initial Energy	3J
4	Transmission power	5.7 x 10e-5
5	Transmission Range	30m
6	Packet size	2kB

Figure 4.7 depicts the signaling cost with respect to the nodes present in Multihoming IoT. The signaling cost is analyzed based on the transport layer model used in research model of Romain *et al.* and Huang et al. It is observed that the signaling cost increases as the number of nodes increases but the proposed incurs much less signaling cost when compared to

other models. The proposed identifier model reduces signaling cost up to 70% with respect to existing models in WSN.

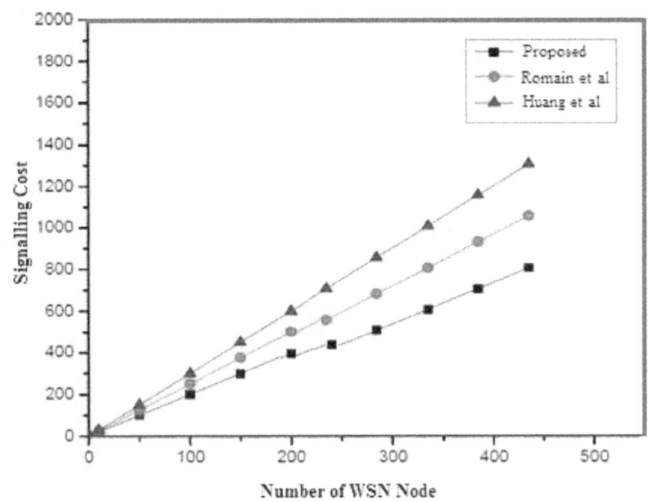

Figure 4.7 Signalling cost comparison based on Number of Nodes

Figure 4.8 depicts the signalling cost based on number of hops and it is observed that when the number of hops increases signalling cost increases for Romain *et al.* and Huang et al. Model and it reduces for proposed model for the same hop values.

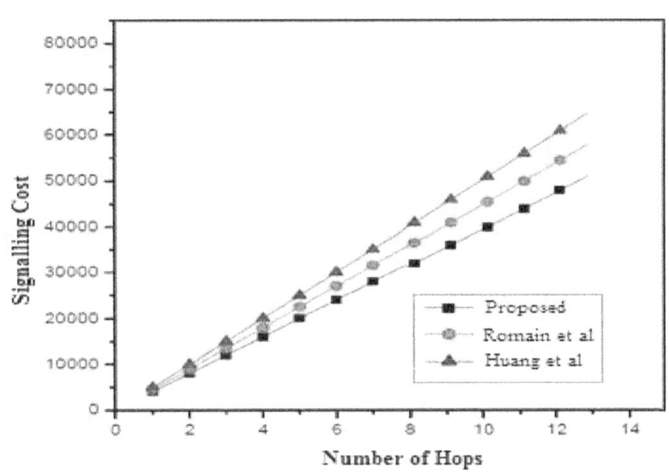

Figure 4.8 Signalling Cost Based On Number of Hops

In that Huang et al model has more signalling cost compared to other models for the same hop values and the proposed model reduced the cost by more than 30% of the actual cost. Figure 4.9 depicts the mobility cost based on number of nodes in the network and it is observed that cost reduces for proposed model when the number of nodes increases.

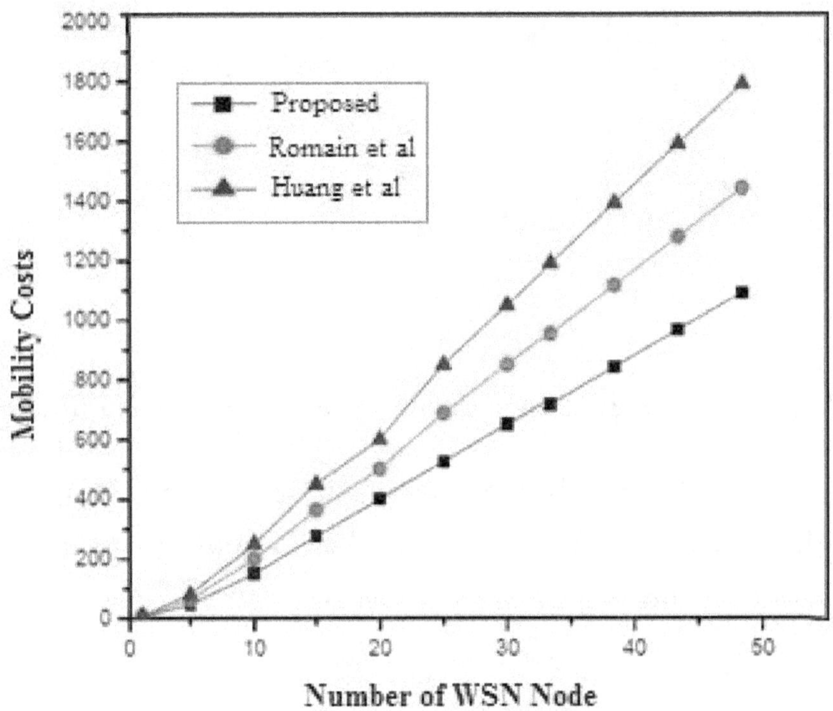

Figure 4.9 Mobility Cost Based On Number of Nodes

For the 50 nodes in the network the cost difference between huang et al model and proposed model varies in the range of 1000 to 1800 with a difference in ratio of 80 %. Figure 4.10 depicts the mobility cost based on number of hops in the network and it is observed that the proposed model provides a minimum mobility for the 10 number of hops in network.

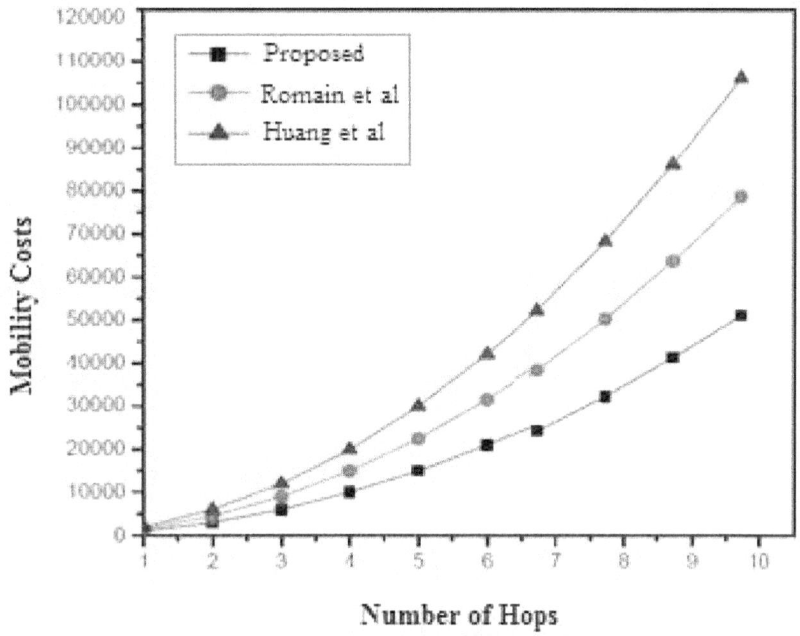

Figure 4.10 Mobility Cost Based On Number of Hops

Figure 4.11 depicts the relationship between the data payload and energy consumption data for the proposed model. Based on the fragmentation boundary value the average energy consumption is calculated for the data payload.

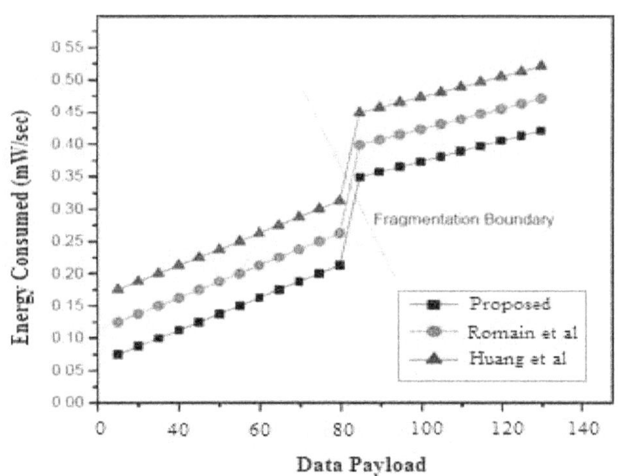

Figure 4.11 Energy Consumption and data payload for proposed model

Table 4.2 describes the performance comparison of proposed model with Romain *et al.* and Huang et al. Model in terms of computation cost and efficiency and error performance.

Table 4.2 Performance Comparison of Proposed model with Romain *et al.* and Huang et al. Model

S.No	Parameter	Romain Et al	Huang Et al	Proposed Model
1	Computation cost (%)	0.026	0.161	0.047
2	Memory Usage	44722	42257	40569
3	Efficiency	67.52%	68.25%	74.56%

Based on the signalling cost and packet delivery ratio the efficiency of the models are calculated and it is observed that proposed model has better performance than the other two models.

4.8 SUMMARY

IoT enables smart applications and services for using sensors, actuators which is identifiable in heterogeneous networks and architectures presented in this chapter. Existing identification schemes and its research challenges are identified based on the proposed format are discussed based on the standard architecture with reference to energy efficiency. The proposed architecture is based on management protocol and efficiency in terms of reducing signaling cost, mobility cost and end to end delay based on the increasing packet delivery ratio. Proposed architecture implementation in IoT domain applications reduces the signalling cost up to 70% and mobility cost by 67% compared to existing models. Based on the transport layer protocol the proposed model increases the packet delivery ratio and end to end ratio into a significant value. Next chapter discuss about the secured routing in multihoming using back propagation neural network (BPNN).

CHAPTER 5

NEURAL NETWORK BASED SECURED ROUTING PROTOCOL IN MULTIHOMING IOT USING DE ALGORITHM

Routing is an essential challenging issue in the wireless sensor network since the performance of system mainly depends on the efficient way of delivering data from one point to another point as destination. The main function of this routing depends on the network layer and it is the third layer in the protocol stack. To make this routing in to efficient one designer must know about the common routing strategies and its effects. Some features in physical layers are asymmetric in nature and communication issues are considered to improve the performance of the system. Design support to routing automatically increases the Quality of service (QoS) with low latency and high delivery ratio. Based on the link quality and the parameters from the lower layers the functionalities and the affecting features, utilization ratio measures must be considered while providing an efficient routing protocol. This is because on each paradigm design measures have its own challenges based on the applications specified by the user. All the issues are classified and categorized into wireless multihop network with unique features. Some basic routing functions and its components are essential in multi hop routing protocol to provide a better solution to the challenges present in wireless sensor networks. This chapter provides an efficient secured routing protocol to the nodes present in multi homing IoT environment by adapting back propagation neural network and adaptive modulation scheme.

5.1 INTRODUCTION

The basic building blocks, while considering the wireless routing protocol, depend on the main function and the message content is important from a source to destination. Route discovery, route representation and route selections are essential in considering the routing models for data forwarding.

5.1.1 Route Discovery

Route discovery is the initial stage in the wireless routing protocol, since the route discovery is a process of finding a set of possible routes between two terminals using other nodes present in the network. The process of finding the route in WSN is broadly classified into three modules as

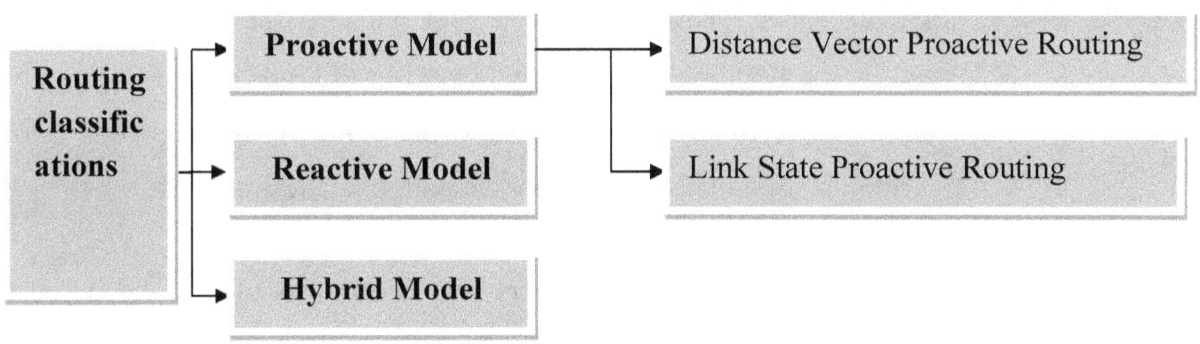

Figure 5.1 Routing classifications used in WSN

Proactive routing is further classified into distance vector routing and link state routing. This two routing modules differ in their network topology based on the information and techniques used to handle the issues in the wireless network particularly in MANET.

Proactive Distance vector routing discovers the routes for the process based on the routing table used. This routing table has all the information about the possible combination of nodes from source to destination and it finds the best path to reach the destination. Based on the information exchanged in the network through neighbours this routing table updates periodically to maintain the topology. The destination list and cost for transmission from one node to another node is available in the information table.

Proactive Link State routing is established as a replacement of distance vector routing since it DV avoids the routing loops and is affected by infinity problem. The main objective of the link state model is to overcome the issues present in DV routing by maintaining a global information topology at each node. In LS routing each node periodically checks the cost from the neighbours for information update and is given as a link state packet. This link state packet prevents the network by flooding based on the flooding procedure followed in the link layer and this process completes based on the cost of all the links in the network. Dijkstra algorithm is used to obtain the shortest path to all destinations.

Reactive route discovery works on basis of demand based route discovery. If a source needs to send information to one destination it must initiate a route discovery process to set up a path that utilizes minimum energy. It performs transmission by requesting permission to all nodes as a broadcast message and once if the destination reacts for the broadcast then the transmission process initiates based on the route reply packet received back to the source. Reactive routing mainly avoids the periodic update process, since due to the periodic update the network becomes overloaded which is considered as an advantage over proactive routing,.

Hybrid routing process is the combination of reactive and proactive technique. It is used to provide an efficient routing by overcoming the limitations of both routing models. It reduces the control overhead in the proactive routing and delays in case of reactive routing.

5.2 SECURITY ISSUES IN MH-IOT

Multi homing IoT has number of security issues due to its mobility nature. The usage of multiple IP address for single host and the addresses are interchangeable and this leads to security issues in multi homing host. Address stealing and address flooding are the two factors identified in the multihoming as a security issue. Address stealing is an attack that takes place at any malicious node when that address is used by some others in the same network. The intension of such attacks are affecting the service to actual user in the denial of service attack. In address flooding malicious node creates many number of unknown node groups to create a belief to the user that intruder has all the details about the network and this mainly causes the unusual traffic in the network. These results the peer nodes to flood the target address with unavoidable traffic. Based on the multi homing models it is easy for an intruder to attack the entire network by introducing this simple peer node concept.

The location update is used in the proactive model to secure the sender information at the target address and all the traffic is directed into somewhere or denial of service depends in the actual need of the attacker. The intruder performance in the wireless network is illustrated in figure 5.2.

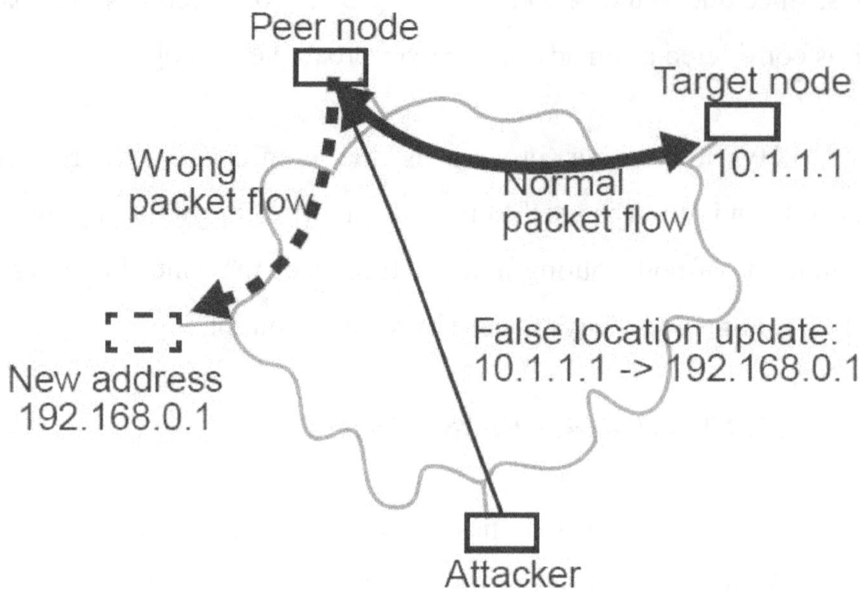

Figure 5.2 Illustration of attacks in WSN

The attack creates a situation to the nodes to check the sender address and its updates based on the new destination. This process leads to information sharing in a wrong way and an unknown destination receives the information instead of authorized node and it reduces the efficiency of the network and also it becomes an excessive load to the third party node. Since if one node receives single wrong information then it is not an issue and in case of receiving a thousands of information from various nodes creates an extra traffic and at the same time it is likely to be as denial of service to users in the network.

5.3 TRANSPORT PROTOCOLS IN MH-IOT

The transport protocol is essential in multihoming IoT and about SCTP and its relations with IPv6 are discussed in chapter three. A short summary is given here to high light the relationship between two SCTP endpoints. In each end point a set of transportation address is created based on the network parameters and numbers on each ports. SCTP has all the transport address and in the end point it must share the same address in practice to identify the non empty set of IP address and single port number. This concept of using pair of address is introduced in the transport layer protocol to receive SCTP packets based on the source and destination IP address. SCTP creates better relationship between two endpoints based on this transport protocol and it comprises of common header and zero chunks. Multiple chunks may be available in some networks since it considers the data and its acknowledgments into a single packet to provide reliable multi stream transport. Figure 5.3 gives an illustration about IoT Protocols used in multi homing applications.

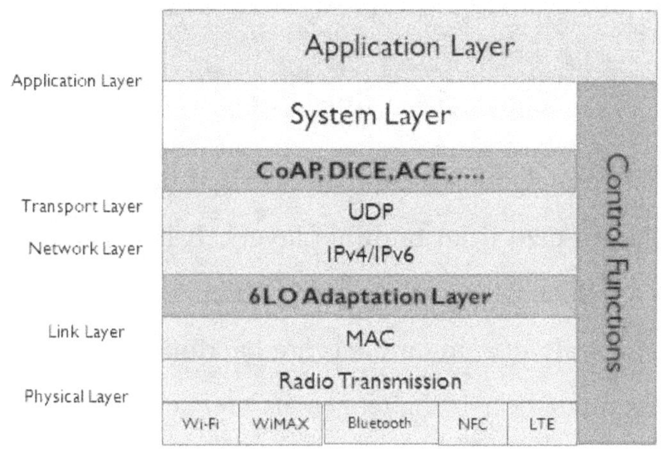

Figure 5.3 IoT Protocol

5.4 PROPOSED HYBRID SECURED ROUTING PROTOCOL (BPNN DE-SRP)

The proposed secure routing model detects the malicious attacks in the networks based on back propagation neural network and differential evolution module. A single layer BPNN consists of input layer, hidden layer and output layer as shown in figure 5.4.

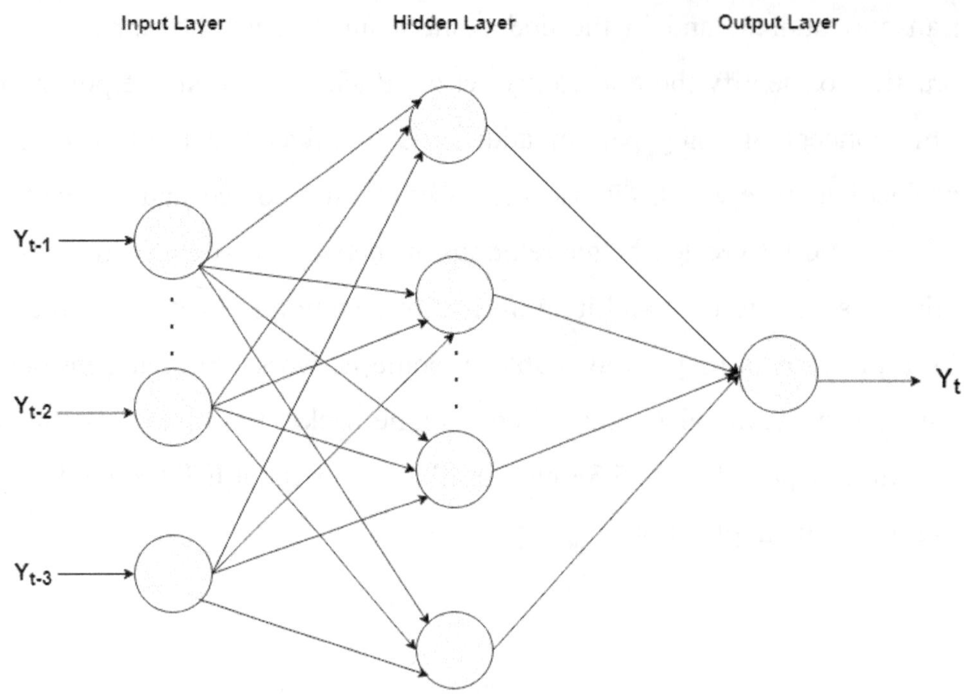

Figure 5.4 illustration of BPNN

Back propagation neural network is a machine learning model works on collected data from multiple layers. It is very useful for analysing large amount of data with high variety which gives analysis for intrusion detection. Large scale learning models are handling large volume of inputs to improve the computational challenges in the network. This raw data is a challenge for data management system in the network for security purposes. It is necessary to adapt the deep learning stream to handle this large volume of raw data in the network.. The input and output layers are linked to each other by means of the hidden layer and the process of update begins with some random weights assigned to each node.

The adjacent layer of BPNN is connected based on the weights and its values are distributed between 1 and -1. Mathematical formulation of system is obtained based on some heuristic approaches proposed by researchers. The efficiency plays a vital role in the WSN since the input nodes and hidden nodes are experimentally verified by trial and error based on the mean square error value of the test data. A single step BPNN is used to forecast the information in the network and based on the present value the target out observations are made and it is represented by an equation

$$\Sigma \qquad (5.1)$$

$$(5.2)$$

Where 'i denotes the input and h denotes the output for the forecasted value at any point, the common connection between the input and hidden layers are given as . is considered as threshold value for hidden layer and output layer respectively and its value is given as 1 and -1 respectively. In all the cases the active function of all the node at each layer is same and an activation function is used in the output layer for linear and non linear function. In order to identify the distortion in the predicted output a logical hyperbolic function is used in the hidden layer as transfer function.

The abnormalities in the network is selected and combined into groups. This group of data is given as input to the neural network to determine the route in the network structure by a group or by an individual. While the mathematical model of neural network is obtained by identifying the distance between the n dimensional input data and output data. By using the lama distance calculation model the distance from data for m and n set is obtained as

$$\sqrt{\qquad} \qquad (5.3)$$

Based on the distance from input data and the neuron the smallest distance and the multiplication factor is considered to find the s dimensional space. The 's' space for two layer is given as

(5.4)

If the smallest point is identified then the vectors are adjusted into the new value based on the equation

Σ – For each (5.5)

Where, k is an integer and it is incremented by 1 for during every iteration of the training process. Represents the neighbourhood radius during iteration t of the training process Represents the vector measures of the neurons at distance from the smallest neuron to others during iterations and respectively

Represents the neighbourhood function

|| || (5.6)

Standard differential evaluation function has four linear operations such as initialization, mutation, crossover and selection.

Initialization deals with the real numbers used in DE for considering several parameters including population size, length, scaling factor and cross over rate. The randomly initiated population is given as

(5.7)

Where i=1,2... N and j=1,2... D and rand is a random variable for uniformly distributed function.

The Mutation process has individual objects based on DE algorithm generated values is given as

(5.8)

Where the serial numbers r1 and r2 are different random variables generated based on the identical objective serial numbers i. the population size is considered based on the scaling factor and it is controlled by the mutation degree in the range of 0 to 2. Crossover operations has an experimental individual value as follows

(5.9)

Where is the randomly generated uniform distribution value and j denoted the gene of an individual. The cross over rate is given as CR and it must fall in the range of 0 to 1 which is defined by the user.

Selection is the last phase in DE algorithm which uses greedy search strategy to adopt the network environment. Each individual objects are used to compete to the corresponding experimental values and it is observed that the fitness value of the experimental is better than the mathematical model. Selecting the suitable fitness function for each method the cost for error function is given as equation follows

(5.10)

The proposed model integrates the routing protocol and intrusion detection system since the secure routing essentially needs anomaly detection starting from input layer to output layer. Based on this input vectors and data packers the number of units in the hidden layer is increased to perform the secure transmission and also to detect the intrusions in the network.

Since the proposed methodology integrates the anomaly detection and misuse detection scheme, we use abnormal packets, which were determined by the anomaly detection scheme, as the input layer.

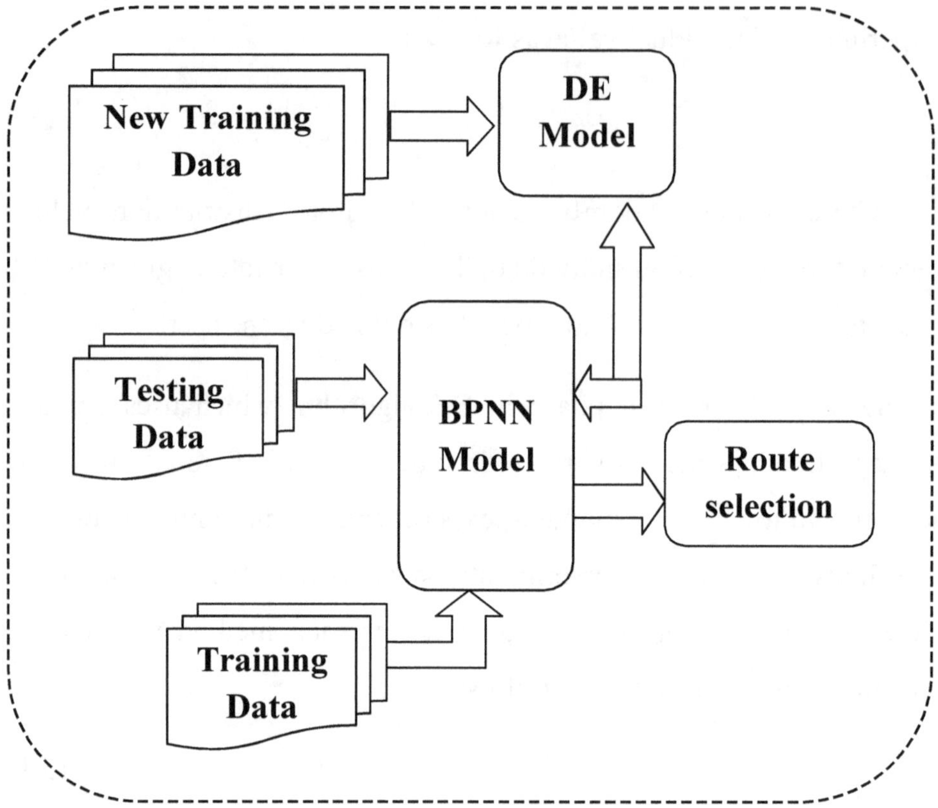

Figure 5.5 Proposed BPNN DE Based Secure Routing and Intrusion Detection System

The number of performing units in input vector is decided by the selected characteristics of the data packets. Furthermore, the number of performing units is included in the hidden layer which is developed by increasing the amount of output layers and the input layers. Performing units in the output layer provide various attacks and a single normal behaviour of the node to decide whether the inserted packet is an attacker or intrusion that forms a classification. The overall process completes when the common data for training and testing completes.

Majority of the data packets in the WSN is cluster based and this makes the training data into an imbalanced one. So BPNN avoids such issue and percolate the training data through hidden layers and also observes the abnormal transmission in the system based on differential evolutionary algorithm. Figure 5.5 provides a description about proposed BPNN DE based secure routing model. It has testing data and training data for all the nodes present in the network and based on the DE algorithm path identification model a suitable path is selected for transmission of data packets from source to destination in the network. BPNN is used to validate the test results and train data which is obtained through DE algorithm.

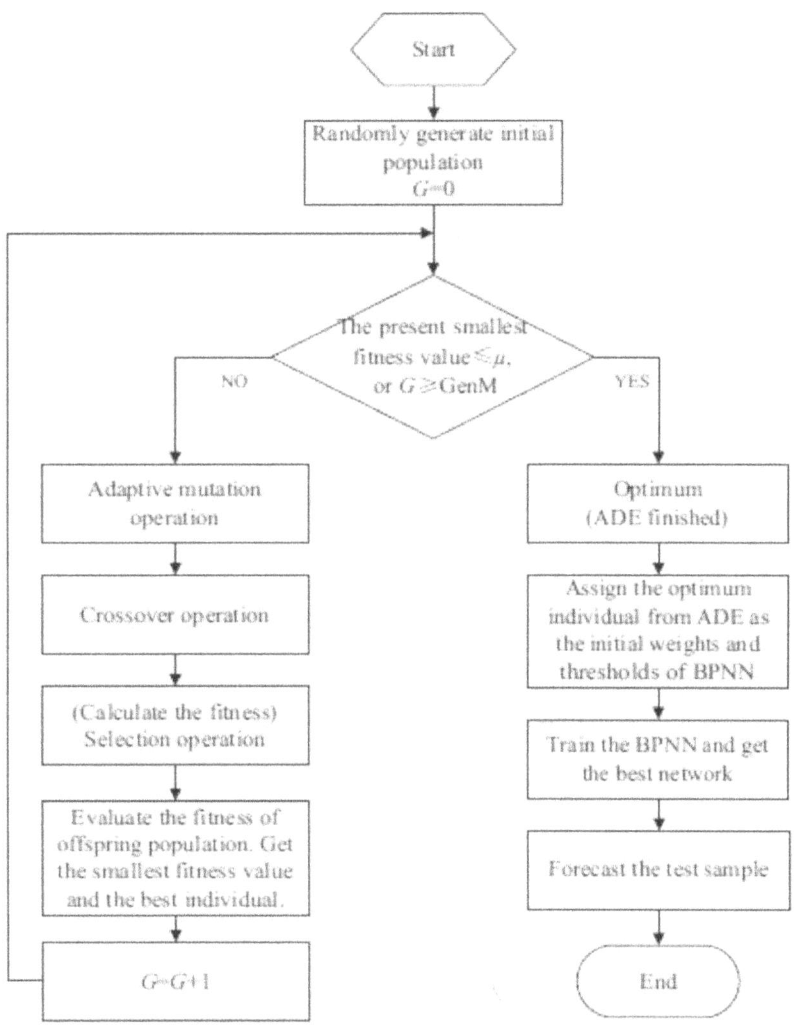

Figure 5.6 Proposed model Process Flow

The process flow of proposed BPNN DE algorithm based routing system is given as process flow in figure 5.6. The process starts from the randomly generated initial population present in the network then based on the fitness function value mutation process takes place and then cross over operation is processed to obtain the cross over rate of the proposed model. The fitness value and the best individual value is obtained and it is given to the BPNN network as optimal values to train the data acquired from the network. A test sample is used to check the results for the proposed experimental model.

5.5 RESULTS AND DISCUSSION

The experimentation in BPNN is based on the hidden layer nodes to achieve the target accuracy and network accuracy. In the training phase the network error is identified for the sample set and for each value classification is performed and it cannot be represented in the network performance. The classification results and training time of target network is calculated using suitable data structures. In the whole process the mean square error of hidden nodes is obtained. The proposed model is tested and experimental results are obtained from the Matlab 14.1 version installed on intel i7 processor with 2.5Ghz frequency. From the experimentation setup and the survey made on various research works the parameters considered in BPNN is listed as follows for analysis.

- Learning Rate
- Initial Weight
- Number of Hidden Units
- Overtraining and Early Stopping Criteria
- Number of Learning Samples
- Activation Function
- Normalization of the Inputs

The performance of the BPNN DE based secure model is analyzed based on the results for the inputs which are processed in MATLAB 14.1. The comparison of learning rate for Train set and Test set are given in table 5.1

Table 5.1 Learning rate for Train set and Test set

Learning Rate	Train set		Test set	
	Loss (%)	Accuracy (%)	Loss (%)	Accuracy (%)
0.1	10.21	87.21	33.21	70.21
0.01	7.96	91.65	21.63	74.65
0.001	8.01	92.31	20.54	78.56
0.0001	7.59	92.01	21.65	73.56
0.00001	7.45	93.24	22.54	72.59

For m data set the proposed BPNN model produces different classification rates and the proposed flow calculates the parameters based on the behavioural pattern in the database. Based on the neural data base and training algorithm the data sets are arranged into groups to train the model for obtaining the suitable route for transmission. Snapshot of the 'Neural network tool' used in the implementation using DE algorithm and MSE criteria for error convergence is depicted in figure 9.

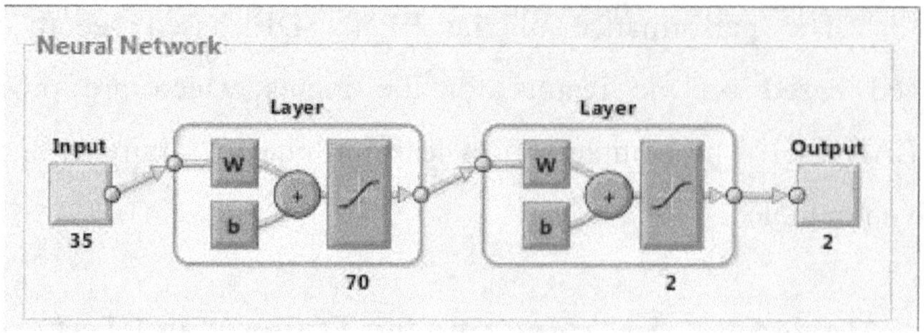

Figure 5.7 Snapshot of NN train tool used in the proposed work

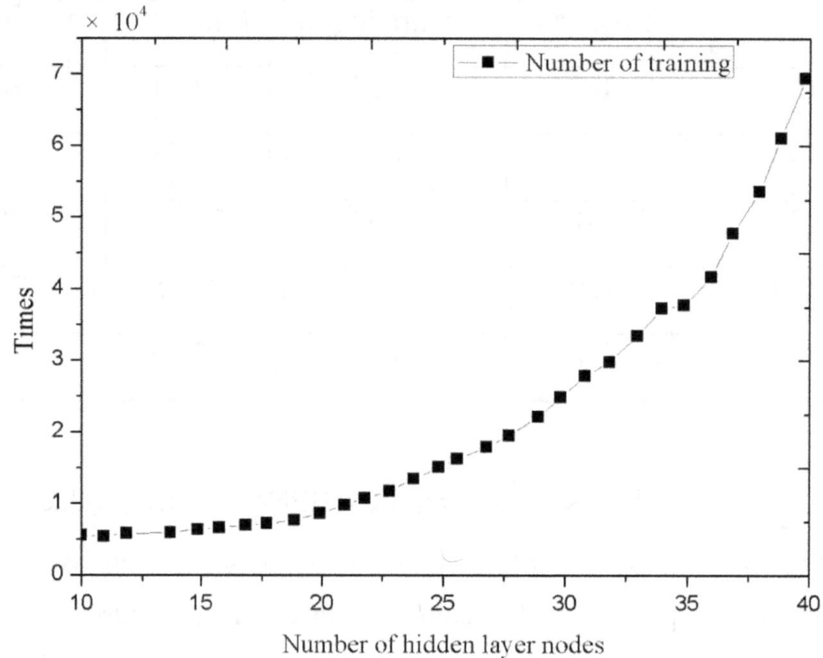

Figure 5.8 Number of hidden layer nodes and computation time comparison

Figure 5.8 depicts the number of hidden layer nodes used in the training process along with the computation time to train the data from 40 nodes. It is observed that the time increases as the hidden layer node increases in terms of 10^4.

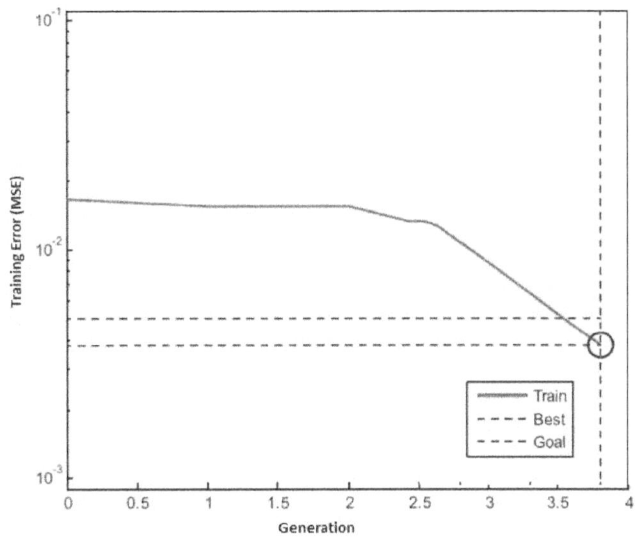

Figure 5.9 Training process of BPNN DE model

Figure 5.9 describes the training process of BPNN to obtain the MSE value for the generation based inputs. In this it is observed that trained value reaches value in between 10^{-1} to 10^{-2} shows that the proposed model has least error value in training phase.

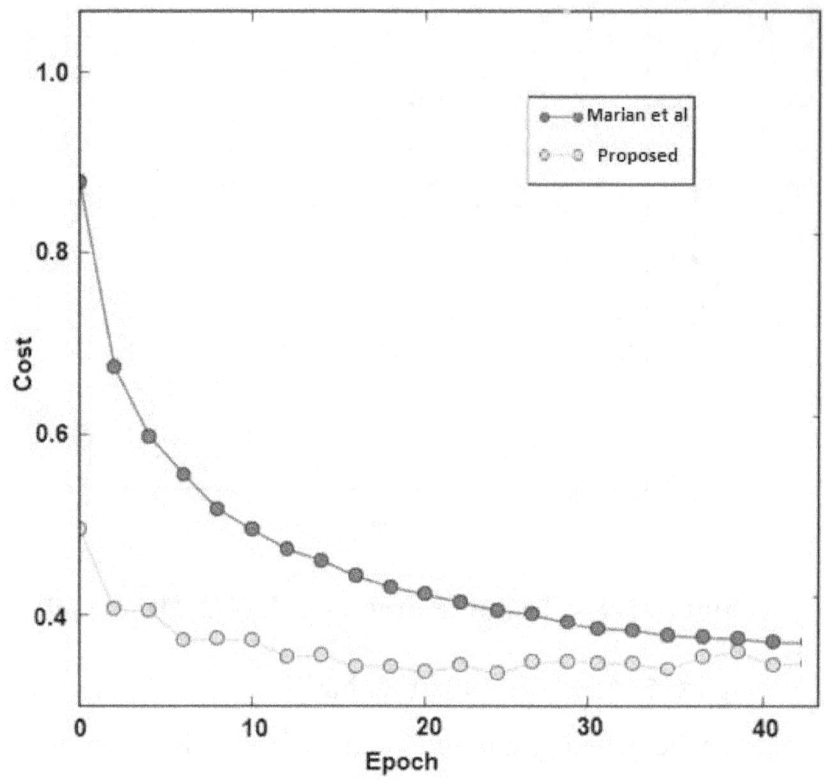

Figure 5.10 Error Convergence plot of proposed model

Figure 5.10 depicts the error convergence for the proposed work is depicted and it could be seen that the proposed method is able to achieve a quicker convergence when compared to existing conventional Marian *et al.* model.

The network is trained for different values of epochs and error goal, where epoch and error goal are training parameters. Typically one epoch of training is defined as a single presentation of all input vectors to the network. The network is then updated according to the results of all those presentations and it is given in figure 5.11.

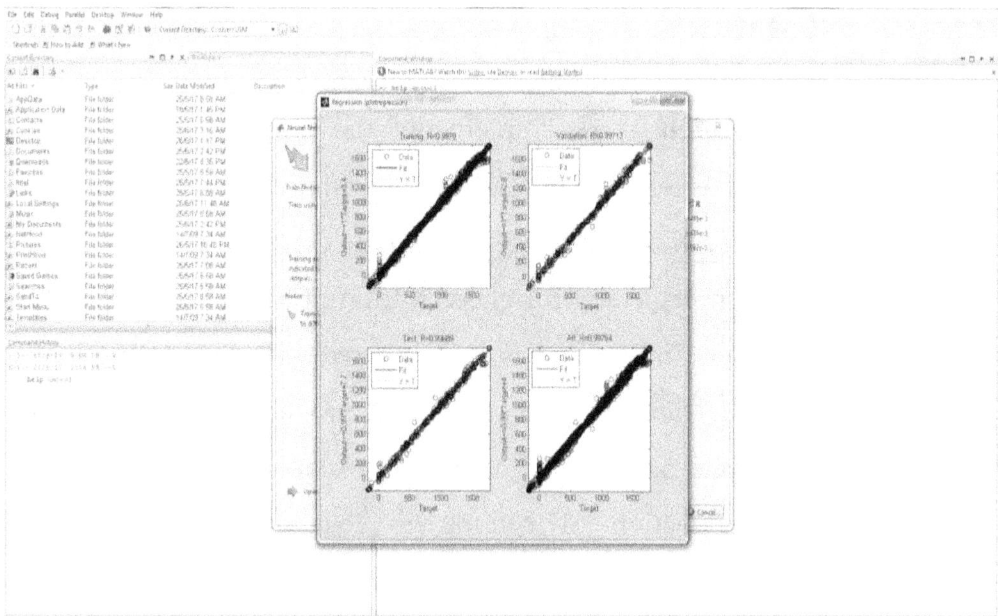

Figure 5.11 Regression Plot for the proposed network

Based on the implementation regression plot is obtained for proposed model with optimum error value of 0.9457e-4 which is considered as good classification rate and the accuracy metrics in routing with different learning rates is tabulated in table 5.2.

Table 5.2 Accuracy Metrics for Different Learning Rates

Learning Rate	Precision (%)	Recall (%)	F -score (%)
0.1	79	72	72
0.01	83	76	72
0.001	84	79	75
0.0001	87	78	75

The performance of the model depends on the learning rate and table 2 depicts the accuracy metrics for the proposed model with different learning rates. The range of the learning rate varies and the precision, recall rate and f score also varies.

5.6 SUMMARY

The research work implements the back propagation neural network along with differential evaluation algorithm to obtain secure routing in multihoming IoT. Network design is obtained from the IoT model and neural network is implemented for classification of available path present in the entire network. DE algorithm is incorporated with BPNN to obtain the secure routing model and intrusion detection model. The proposed model has classification rate as 90% and meets the requirements of user in the network. The introduction of routing in IoT puts forward the data classification under many computing applications. Followed by this research next chapter 6 describes about an optimization model using Ant colony optimization for improving the routing methodology in multi homing IoT network.

CHAPTER 6

MULTIHOMING ACO-MDV ROUTING FOR MAXIMUM POWER EFFICIENCY TO SUPPORT INTERNET OF THINGS

Multi homing routing is essential in IoT application since the usage of multi path is increased day by day. Due to the advancement of recent technologies numerous applications use data transfer technology, mobility and bandwidth allocation based on the available routes to the user is essential in order to satisfy the user requirements. To select a proper channel or path in the network previous chapter proposed a neural network based path selection protocol and this chapter deals with optimization of secured protocol using ant colony optimization and Multipath Distance Vector (MDV) routing strategy to improve network performance,.

6.1 INTRODUCTION

Multihoming is comprised of large number of users in a network which are distributed all over the physical IoT environment. The main objective of IoT is to provide services like monitoring activities, information exchanges and other value added services to mankind for better living environment. IoT act as a common platform for providing smart environment, smart healthcare, smart energy management, intelligent transport, smart agriculture, smart e-governance and other manufacturing product oriented services. It is used to develop an environment of better utility of resources to all users which are present in the network. The overall term defines it as a single term literally as smart city. Figure 6.1 depicts the components in the IoT environment for smart management.

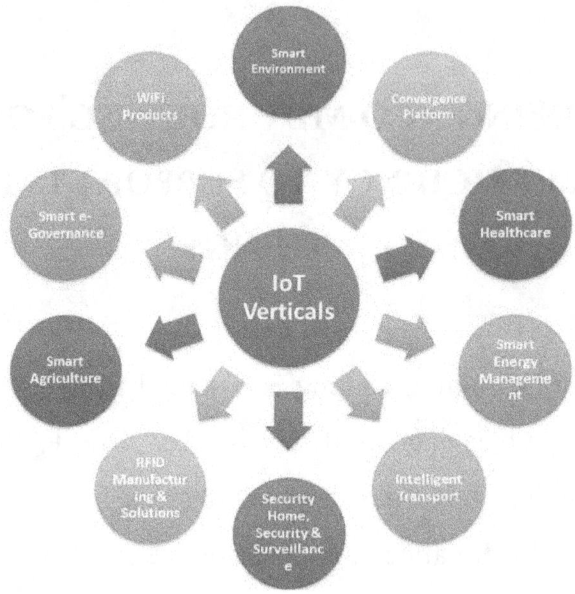

Figure 6.1 Components in Internet of Things (IoT)

The impact of IoT is present everywhere, not only in the smart city but also in every business and it is used as a connecting device to the entire system under a single roof. It helps in business to obtain the gain efficiency; harness intelligence based on wide range of equipments and based on the analysis a customer satisfaction idea can be obtained. The public safety, transportation and other terminals are included in smart industries based on IoT depends upon the three factors such as communication, control and cost saving. Communication performs the transfer of information about the people and the systems from sensors and other informational devices.

The users in this environment are not to be limited in the present environment in the fast moving world. So providing services to that kind of users is necessary in order to provide the better services with quality.

Multihoming concept helps to solve the issues which are discussed above. The simple concept in multihoming is to provide continuous services without disconnecting into the network. So a multiple network is implemented for multiple users and all the users are connected via an IP based protocol. To achieve this concept redundant links are used in the external connectivity through multiple layers of protocols and interfaces. The connection establishment is based on single ISP or multiple ISPs.

The advantage in using this multihoming is that it will provide a dedicated service line to users via one or more ISPs and therefore it makes the network into a balanced load network with less congestion. Second the users are provided with minimum of two ISPs so that if the traffic is less in the network then user can avail the maximum bands and it increases the overall throughput. In the two links if any one of them fails to provide still other line is active and it maintains the connectivity so that the network has less redundancy. Transport protocol is used in the network for multiple addressing which is used in the multiple access control (MAC) network. In most of the cases Internet Protocol (IP) is used to setting up the gateway for normal and business oriented applications and also in smart cities. Figure 6.2 depicts a illustrative example for multihoming.

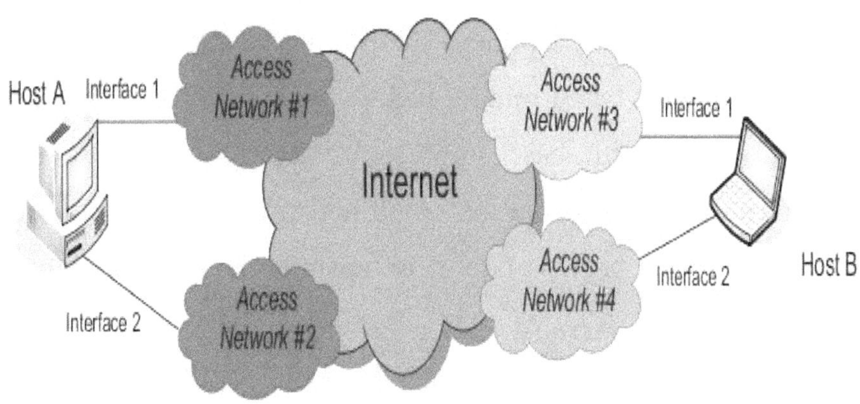

Figure 6.2 Multihoming in wireless Networks

In the wireless sensor network computing the information is a centralized process with low data rate. Multi hop routing and low power nodes are self organizing in nature and data cannot be sent directly from source to the destination.

6.2 ROUTING PROTOCOLS AND ISSUES

Multi hop topology has travel to through the sensor nodes and the routing is based on the three factors such as routing based on the network structure, based on the protocol operation and based on finding the destination. In this routing based on structure includes flat based routing in every node involving in the route formation. In the location based routing sensor nodes are used to find the signal strength parameter through global positioning system. In the protocol based routing, the selection of path among multiple routes is performed by compromising the energy resources. It is a query based routing which is used between the sender and receiver to eliminate the high level of data redundancy. Next routing strategy is the destination based proactive type protocol which uses decision as a tool to select the path in the network. It is hybrid type of protocol that offers mixing of proactive and reactive protocols. Routing based on the communication initiator is another category which uses request as a tool to decide the communication process. Last one is the routing based on the neighbourhood node and it is content based routing focuses mainly about the route selection. The general probabilistic based routing protocols use these neighbourhood nodes for data transmission in the entire network for successful delivery of information or if the process fails it retransmits the dropped packets to the destination again.

The issue in wireless network is power efficiency and security apart from the efficient reliable communication. The main factor to be considered while designing the routing protocol is energy because in the multihoming all the users are to be in the wireless environment and the total power efficiency is a necessary fact while developing the architecture.

6.3 OPTIMIZATION OF ROUTING USING ACO-MDV

The communication system in the multihoming IoT is classified into wireless section and wired section and the wireless section is used as end system that delivers or receives data from the remote content server present in the next network. The remote content server which is used in the wireless networks are mainly focuses the delivery content from control centre to the terminal and the other unnecessary request are not considered in this case particularly in video and data streaming operations. The survey work presents various issues in the wireless multihoming IoT and the claiming the faster transmission than the other algorithms is necessary for effective utilization of services provided in the smart environment.

The proposed protocol is based on the standard MDV (Multipath Distance Vector) protocol and supported by the ACO principles. ACO is inspired by the behaviour of ant species which is their regular process. The ants deposit pheromones on the ground in order to make their nest and the path is assigned for the other members in that family, so that they can access the path to have food and also to store the food in that particular location. Additionally separate dangerous paths are also identified by the ants to avoid the threats and other issues. Since it optimizes the path the capable of solving the discrete and combinational problems in the optimization process can be converged easily when compared to other optimization techniques.

To illuminate the basic principle of ACO, let us consider the paths and of Figure 6.3 between a nest and a food source as an example. Furthermore, let us denote that and are the number of ants along the paths and path respectively at the time step , and and are the probability of choosing path and path , respectively. Then, the probability of an ant choosing path at the time step is given by

[] (6.1)

(6.2)

Where z is the degree of attraction of an unexplored branch and is the bias towards using pheromone deposits in the decision process.

If the new position is identified based on random distribution then an observation process starts for the stability

(6.3)

If the stability of position is better than the present position and the new position is updated.

( ) (6.4)

The above steps are repeated many number of times and it is frequently updated. ACO is changed as an increased percentage in terms of distance between the present position and new position for every displacement. If the better place is not identified after performing the above steps it move with a random step. In all possible iteration the swarm changes its place from previous to present position. To follow the behaviour of AF forward movement for one step is given as

( ) (6.5)

Position of AFi follows the best . So that the ACO i moves randomly and this follow behaviour results in increased convergence rate.

The interaction behaviour between them is done globally. The Euclidean distance is calculated among all the ants for detecting neighbours distance. For effective improvement in convergence rate the possibility of reducing the computational load must be done in all cases.

The centre which is obtained previously is calculated based on the intra cluster. The function is minimum and it is given as

$$(\qquad) \Sigma \qquad (\iint \| \quad - \|) \tag{6.6}$$

where the new cost facility is essential for identification of minimum requirements with acceleration constants.

An ant chooses between the path and path using the following decision rule: if then choose path , otherwise choose path . Here, is a random number having an uniform distribution in the range of [0, 1]. ACO performs well in the dynamic and distributed routing problems of WSNs.

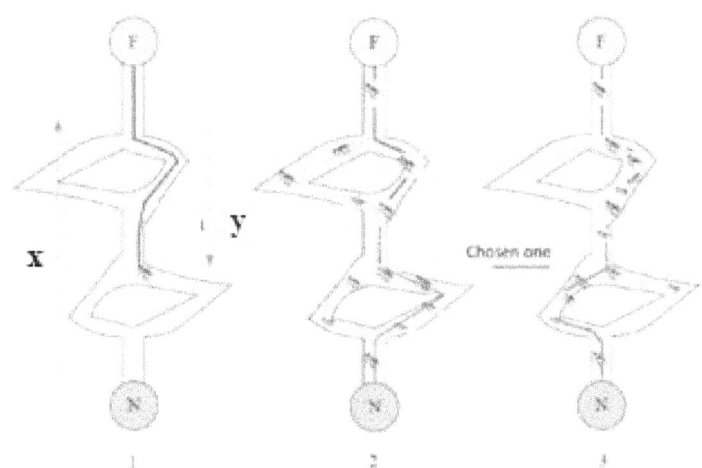

Figure 6.3 Illustration of ant colony optimization

The standard process includes the packet size and frequency of occurrence, contraction coefficient parameter, follows and prey behaviour. In the prey behaviour the individual independent movements are considered from one place to other place. If ACO of is moved to new location the following actions must takes place.

The metrics used in the neighbour home selection are hop count, average link present in the rout and finally average load of the route. The routing tables are used to maintain the dynamic changing nature of the routing and also for the quality of services. In general the protocol works in three stages and it is compared and included in the ant colony optimization for better routing model. Link discovery process, link maintenance process and failure handling process are the process and in that the last failure handling process is performed by using missing acknowledgement technique.

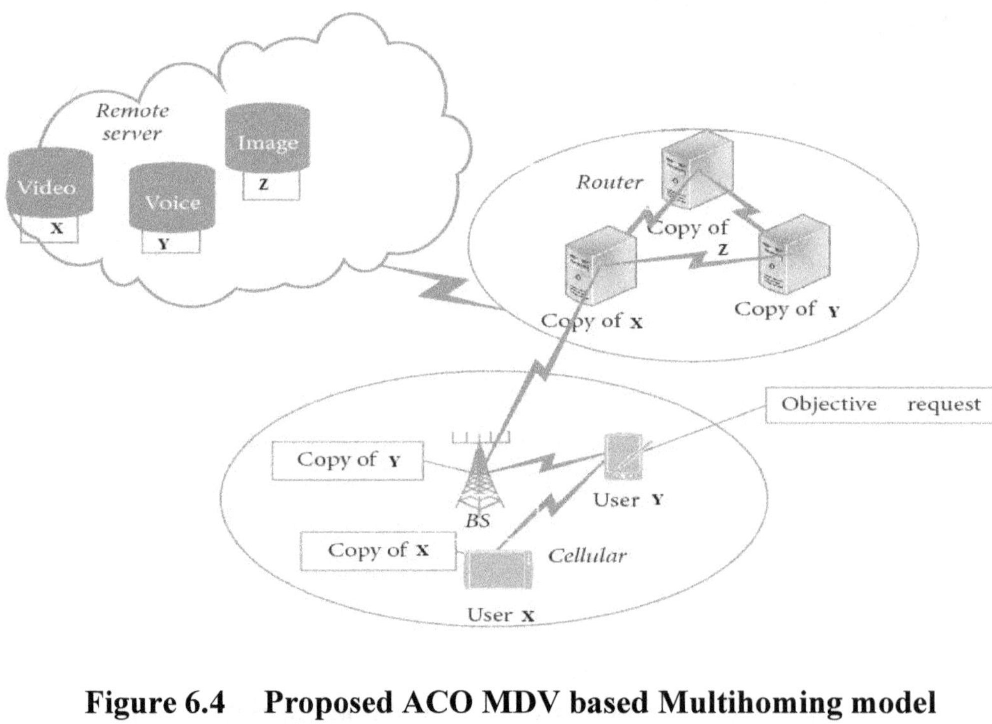

Figure 6.4 Proposed ACO MDV based Multihoming model

The protocol works in three phases i.e. route discovery phase, route maintenance and the route failure handling phase. The failure management is done through missing acknowledgement technique. Figure **6.4** is a general illustration of multihoming model used in the IoT environment. In the proposed model the ant colony optimization is combined with multipath distance vector routing to define the better routing methodology in the wireless sensor networks to attain the maximum efficiency in the multihoming IoT environment. The short summary of algorithm for the proposed model to calculate the minimum energy consumption to calculate the power efficiency is described as follows:

Algorithm for minimum energy consumption Based on ant colony optimization on demand multipath distance vector (ACO-MDV) routing

---

[illegible]

[illegible]

6.4 RESULTS AND DISCUSSION

The proposed model ant colony optimization on demand multipath distance vector (ACO-MDV) is performed in network simulator NS-2 with two ground models. The performance measures are discussed by measuring approximately 80 simulations. The number of networks and the relay nodes are increased in the scale based on the number of users and produces large number of possible paths and are used to determine the shortest path with better power efficiency in the regions.

The communication radius is increased if the users are increased and it is decreased if the users are reduced. Based on the nodes and availability of accessing path the energy efficient routing is processed in IoT. Simulation results tell that ACO-MDV performance is more or less improved as compared to the other two algorithms in terms of above said metrics. To make the proposed algorithm more suitable for IoT applications the energy level of each network is checked and the selects the transmission process based on the largest extent. In these dynamic algorithm based on the efficient routing the network operation varies dynamically and reduces the network overhead.

Table 6.1 Performance metrics used in proposed model

S.No	Metrics	Value
1	Network size	500m x 500m
2	Initial Energy	6oomJ
3	Pd	150mJ
4	Data aggregation energy cost	75pj/bit j
5	Packet size	4200 bit
6	Data Rate	Variable
7	Interface type	Wireless physical interface
8	Mobility speed	1to 20 m/s
9	Mobility Model	Random type

Table 6.1 depicts the parameter comparisons of proposed model. it defines the entire network area and the initial energy so that after implementing the proposed routing algorithm the results have to be compared.

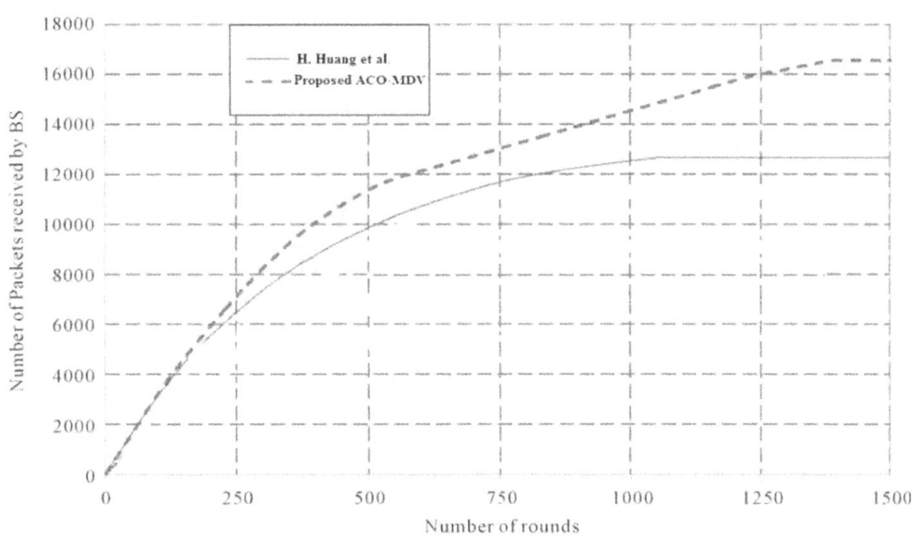

Figure 6.5 Number of rounds vs packet delivered

The number of rounds the process performed to measure the metric is depicted in figure 6.5. In this the number of packets are considered for the proposed model and the H.Huang et al model and from the figure it is observed that the proposed model has high value than the hung model.

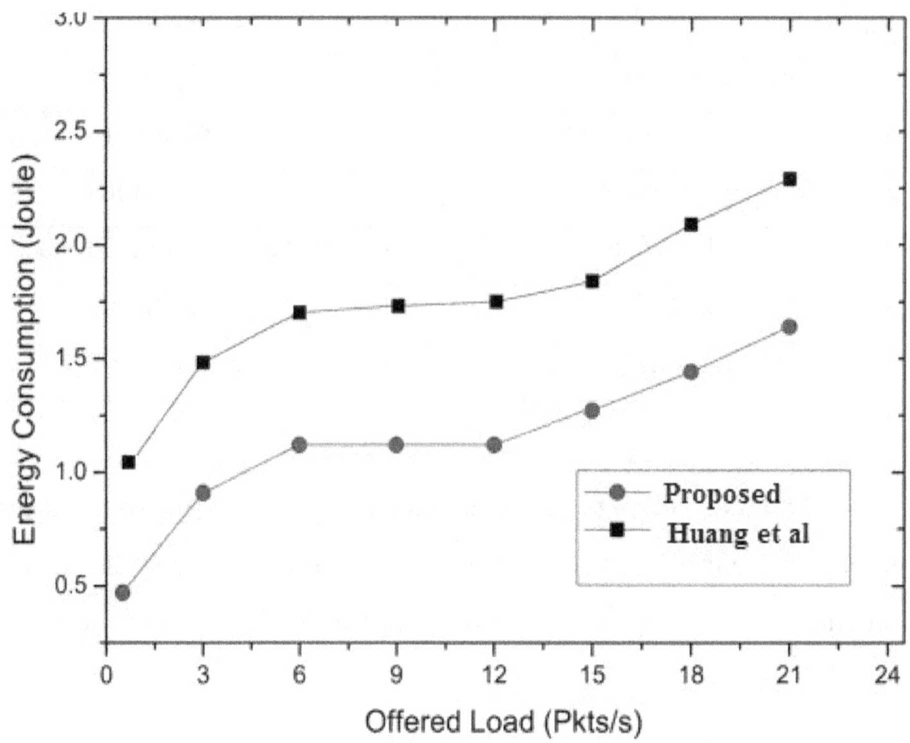

Figure 6.6 Energy Consumption against load in the network

The offered load decides the energy consumed by the network is in figure 6.6 and the process is compared along with the H.huang model. From the observation the proposed model delivers more packets compared to other model and the energy consumed is also less for the same cases. Table 6.2 depicts the computation time and power efficiency factor for both the models.

Table 6.2 Performance comparison

S.No	Parameter	H.Huang et al	Proposed model
1	Computation Time	224ms	165ms
2	Power Efficiency	78.45%	89.14%
3	Error convergence	0.0564	0.0001

Figure 6.7 depicts the computation time and power efficiency comparison for the proposed model and H.Huang et al model. From this observation the proposed model used less time to compute the packets transfer and connection establishment time and power efficiency is also less than the other model.

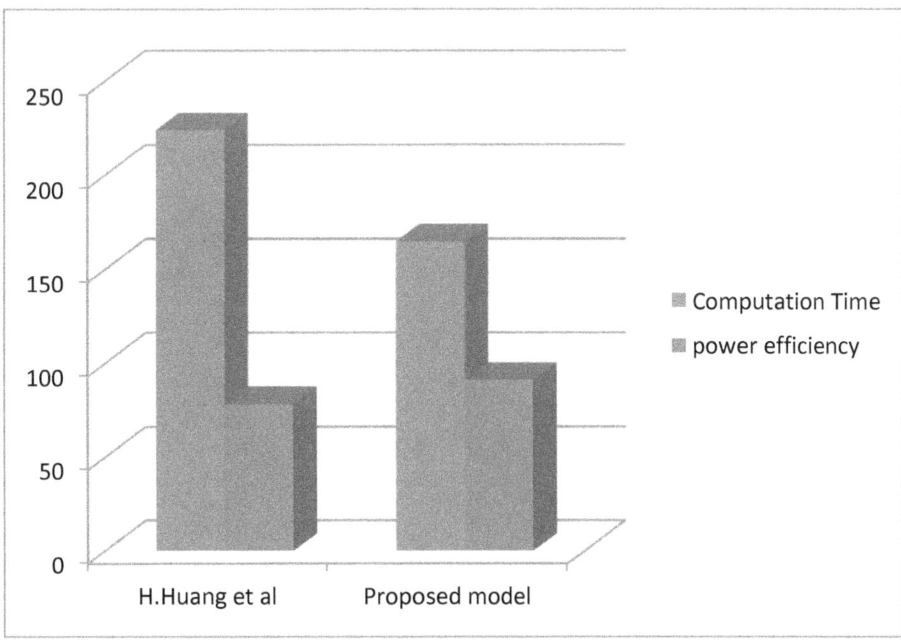

Figure 6.7 performance comparison

Table 6.3 Performance comparison with other standard Models

S.NO	PROTOCOL	LIFE TIME	RESIDUAL ENERGY	TOTAL ENERGY CONSUMPTION
1	LEACH	1578	2167	2167
2	EE-LEACH	2226	3153	3170
3	SEEN	2316	2789	2790
4	LEACH-C	1736	2322	2623
5	O-LEACH	2078	2772	2772
6	LEACH-M	1937	2392	2675
7	IEE-LEACH	2636	3242	3242
8	H.HUANG ET AL	2701	3346	3346
9	PROPOSED MODEL	2786	3456	3456

Figure 6.8 depicts the life time, Residual energy and Total energy consumption for the proposed model with the standard models. From this observation the proposed model give more life time and minimum energy consumption with other models.

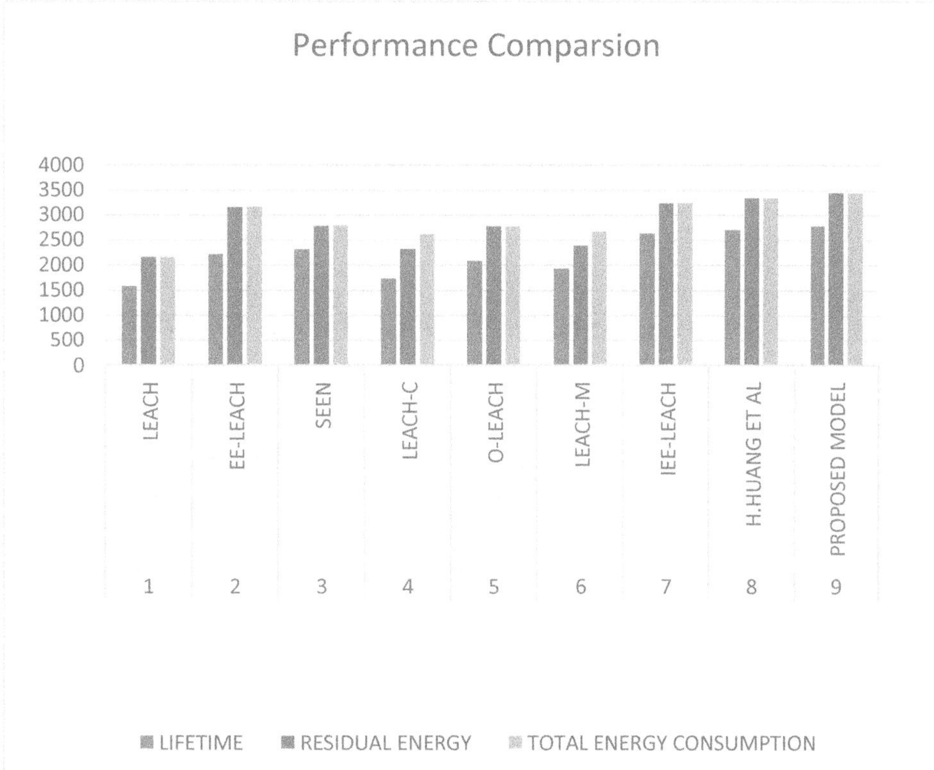

Figure 6.8 performance comparison with standard models

6.5 SUMMARY

Form the results the proposed ant colony optimization multipath distance vector routing produces better results than the huang et.al. Model in terms of energy, computation time, and error convergence factors. This proposed routing algorithm supports multihoming IoT environment than the conventional routing algorithms which are presently used in the wireless sensor networks.

CHAPTER 7

CONCLUSION AND FUTURE SCOPE

The research work in this dissertation have addressed various issues in multi homing IoT applications and proposed an optimal algorithm for secure and efficient routing in WSN. Due to day by day increase of communication protocols and the usage of smart applications creates on demand to the service providers to find new algorithms to satisfy the user needs. This chapter presents the summary of work done with the findings from experimentations and also includes the limitations and its future scope of this research work.

7.1 SUMMARY OF THE WORK DONE

The objective of the thesis is to design and implement an optimal secured routing mechanism to provide efficient routing in the wireless sensor network. To start with various literatures an extensive survey has been made to define the parameters and its issues in WSN and IoT applications. Survey of literature has been carried on to define the various routing protocols and its limitations. Different routing strategies are obtained from research articles and the proposed evaluation is based on the optimization model studied from the literature. The proposed model algorithm has features of selecting suitable path to transfer data from one node to other node which helps the service provider to serve all the users in the network. The last part of this chapter brings a clear idea about the issues and challenges in the multi homing communication and in particular IoT based applications.

The next part of the thesis provides an insight about the basic concepts of multihoming and its models which are appropriate classes based on its features. A detailed elaboration of various routing models have been briefed with suitable illustrations with emphasis on green routing which tends to improve energy conservation. The chapter further emphasizes the role of multi homing in IoT and the various transport and management protocols necessary for the multihoming implementation.

The experimental work commences in the subsequent chapter by defining a heterogeneous multi homed ETSI machine to machine architecture which identifies the different functionalities and entity points in the framework. ETSI is a distributed system capable of operating in the network level and local level. The proposed architecture is implemented in MATLAB and the performance of the proposed model have been compared with the reference model taken from the literature. Comparison is based on parameters such as sensor nodes and hop counts. Observation of signalling cost computed in the network reports 70% reduction when compared with the conventional models. Another parameter computed is the mobility costs which have reported 80% improvement when the cost varies from 1000 to 1800 for a fixed node count of 50. Energy consumption has been computed and compared against varying payload sizes with two different conventional methods and proposed model exhibits reduced energy levels.

The proposed model has been optimized using a supervised learning algorithm in the form of neural network for improving the security issues of the proposed routing protocol. Various security issues have been discussed and solution is proposed using a back propagation neural network model in a hybrid combination with DESRP to implement the proposed secure routing and intrusion detection mechanism. Experimental analysis presents illustrations for observed parameters like learning rate, number of hidden units, learning samples and normalization. An accuracy of nearly 70% is proposed with a learning rate of 0.1and the error convergence plot depicts a quick computation time in the form of early convergence when compared with existing routing techniques.

The final chapter presents an evolutionary and nature inspired algorithm in the form of ant colony algorithm to optimize the power efficiency and maximize the same to support its compatibility with IoT applications. Ant colony algorithm is an optimization technique which is based on the food foraging behaviour of ants which have been discussed with elaborate illustrations. The proposed optimization algorithm is tested for its efficiency in terms of energy consumption against varying packet size and an optimal computation time of 165ms is reported justifying the efficiency of proposed work. A maximum power efficiency of nearly 89% is observed in the experimentation process thus making the proposed model to be an ideal model when implemented over heterogeneous machine to machine multi homing models.

7.2 LIMITATIONS OF THE WORK

Internet of Things (IoT) offers a huge potential to be tapped for accessing and transfer of data to and from the cloud networks with great ease. On the other hand, since data is movement through wireless medium, there is a great deal of threat from hackers and attack nodes which may introduce malicious packets of information which may infect other packets. One such renowned attack in in case of IoT is the distributed denial of service attack (DDoS) which causes congestion and traffic related issues in the communication path. Hence appropriate network attack defence mechanisms should be incorporated into the system to address such issues.

Another limitation observed with respect to internet of things is the nature of nodes which form the back bone of the IoT implementations. The nodes could be static or dynamic with each configuration having its own merits and demerits. However, the effect of dynamic topology is more pronounced as it causes the central controlling system to continuously monitor the geography and topology of the network and adjust the configuration parameters accordingly. In such cases, adaptability and its optimization play a vital role in defining the efficiency of the implementation.

Another limitation is on the number of nodes actively involved in the multihoming environment against the total energy consumed by the network. Every node has its own energy consumption which has to be optimized to reduce the overall energy consumption leading towards green computing. Hence, decision on optimal number of nodes to cover the required application areas are high desirable and critical in implementation of the network.

7.3 FUTURE SCOPE

Internet of things (IoT) have immense capabilities and potentials which need to be tapped to implement state of the art future generation networks where all processes are digitized and automated. Apart from the proposed work in this thesis, IoT pose several prospects ranging from remote monitoring and control in patient health care, smart home, smart farms, smart cities etc. They also offer an excellent choice for network backups with one network being used as the primary channel and the other network used for network backup of information and data.

Research in multi homing networks offer a wide scope in gaming industry where the developed product could be released through multiple networks the process which is also alternately termed as multi-platformed. This could boost the promotional activities of the concern launching the product and help improve its sales efficiency.

REFERENCES

1. Aditya Akella; Bruce Maggs; Srinivasan Seshan; Anees Shaikh (2008), 'On the Performance Benefits of Multihoming Route Control' IEEE/ACM Transactions on Networking, Vol.16, No.1, Pp.91 – 104

2. Al-Ali R.; Imran A. Zualkernan; Mohammed Rashid; Ragini Gupta; MazinAlikarar (2017), 'A smart home energy management system using IoT and big data analytics approach' IEEE Transactions on Consumer Electronics, Vol.63, No. 4, Pp. 426 - 434

3. Alejandro Ribeiro; Nikolaos D. Sidiropoulos; Georgios. B. Giannakis (2008), 'Optimal Distributed Stochastic Routing Algorithms for Wireless Multihop Networks' IEEE Transactions on Wireless Communications, Vol.7, No.11, Pp. 4261 – 4272

4. Alessandro Arsie; KetanSavla; Emilio Frazzoli (2009), 'Efficient Routing Algorithms for Multiple Vehicles with no Explicit Communications' IEEE Transactions on Automatic Control, Vol.54, No.10, Pp. 2302 – 2317

5. Ali RızaEkti; Xu Wang; Muhammad Ismail; ErchinSerpedin; Khalid A. Qaraqe (2016) , 'Joint User Association and Data-Rate Allocation in Heterogeneous Wireless Networks' IEEE Transactions on Vehicular Technology, Vol.65, No. 9, Pp.7403 – 7414

6. Andres Mejia; Maurizio Palesi; JosÉFlich; Shashi Kumar; Pedro Lopez; Rickard Holsmark; JosÉDuato (2009), 'Region-Based Routing: A Mechanism to Support Efficient Routing Algorithms in NoCs' IEEE Transactions on Very Large Scale Integration (VLSI) Systems, Vol. 17, No.3, Pp. 356 – 369

7. Antonio Caruso; Stefano Chessa; Soledad Escolar; Xavier del Toro; Juan Carlos López (2018), 'A Dynamic Programming Algorithm for High-Level Task Scheduling in Energy Harvesting IoT' IEEE Internet of Things Journal, Vol.5, No.3, Pp. 2234 – 2248

8. ArseniyVitkovskiy; VassosSoteriou; ChrysostomosNicopoulos (2013), 'Dynamic fault-tolerant routing algorithm for networks-on-chip based on localised detouring paths' IET Computers & Digital Techniques, Vol.7, No.2, Pp. 93 – 103

9. Asad Abbas; Isma Farah Siddiqui; Scott Uk–Jin Lee; Ali Kashif Bashir; WaleedEjaz; Nawab Muhammad Faseeh Qureshi (2018),

'Multi-Objective Optimum Solutions for IoT-Based Feature Models of Software Product Line' IEEE Access, Vol. 6, Pp.12228 – 12239

10. Auon Muhammad Akhtar; Mohammad Reza Nakhai; A. Hamid Aghvami (2013), 'On the Use of Cooperative Physical Layer Network Coding for Energy Efficient Routing' IEEE Transactions on Communications, Vol. 62, No.4, Pp. 1498 – 1509

11. Avijit Mathura, Thomas Newea, WalidElgenaidia, MuzaffarRaoa, Gerard Doolya, Daniel Toal (2017), 'A secure end-to-end IoT solution' Journal of Sensors and Actuators-Elsevier, No.263, pp.291–299.

12. Baoxian Zhang; JieHao; Hussein T. Mouftah (2014|), 'Bidirectional Multi-Constrained Routing Algorithms' IEEE Transactions on Computers, Vol. 63, No.9, Pp. 2174 – 2186

13. Bruno P. Santos, LuizF.M. Vieira, MarcosA.M. Vieira (2017), 'CGR: Centrality-based green routing for Low-power and Lossy Networks' Journal of Computer Networks- Elsevier, No. 129, pp.117–128.

14. Catalina Aranzazu-Suescun; MihaelaCardei (2017),'Distributed algorithms for event reporting in mobile-sink WSNs for Internet of Things' Tsinghua Science and Technology, Vol.22, No.4, Pp. 413 – 426

15. CesareAlippi; RomoloCamplani; Manuel Roveri (2009), 'An Adaptive LLC-Based and Hierarchical Power-Aware Routing Algorithm' IEEE Transactions on Instrumentation and Measurement, Vol.58, No. 9, Pp. 3347 – 3357

16. Chang R. S.;. Lin C. F (2007), 'Using link layer throughput maximisation in ad hoc network routing algorithms' IET Communications, Vol.1, No. 5, Pp. 875 – 879

17. Chris Jackson, Simon J. Hollis (2011), 'A deadlock-free routing algorithm for dynamically reconfigurable Networks-on-Chip' Microprocessors and Microsystems, Vol. 35,Pp. 139–151

18. Chuah S.-P, Z. Chen, Y.-P. Tan (2013), 'Energy minimization for wireless video transmissions with deadline and reliability constraints', IEEE Trans. Circuits Syst. Video Technol., vol. 23, No. 3, pp. 467-481.

19. Chung-Ming Huang; Ming-Sian Lin; Lik-Hou Chang (2010), 'The Design of Mobile Concurrent Multipath Transfer in Multihomed Wireless Mobile Networks' The Computer Journal, Vol.53, No.10, Pp. 1704 – 1718.

20. Claudia Archetti , Elena Fernández , Diana L. Huerta-Muñoz (2017), 'The Flexible Periodic Vehicle Routing Problem' Computers and Operations Research, Vol. 85, Pp. 58–70

21. Daniel Minoli; KazemSohraby; Benedict Occhiogrosso (2017), 'IoT Considerations, Requirements, and Architectures for Smart Buildings—Energy Optimization and Next-Generation Building Management Systems' IEEE Internet of Things Journal, Vol. 4, No.1, Pp. 269 – 283

22. Daniel Wallace T.; AbdallahShami (2012), 'A Review of Multihoming Issues Using the Stream Control Transmission Protocol' IEEE Communications Surveys & Tutorials, Vol.14, No.2, pp. 565 – 578.

23. Dimitris C. Paraskevopoulos, Gilbert Laporte, Panagiotis P. Repoussis, Christos D. Tarantilis (2017), ' Resource constrained routing and scheduling: Review and research prospects', European Journal of Operational Research-Elsevier, No. 263, pp.737–754

24. Donghyuk Han; Jong-Moon Chung (2014), 'Self-Similar Traffic End-to-End Delay Minimization Multipath Routing Algorithm' IEEE Communications Letters, Vol.18, No. 12, Pp. 2121 – 2124

25. DrissiM. , M. Oumsis, and D. Aboutajdine (2016), 'A Fuzzy AHP Approach to Network Selection Improvement in Heterogeneous Wireless Networks,' Springer Int. Publ. AG 2016, Vol. 1, Pp. 169–182.

26. Emma Fitzgerald; MichałPióro; ArturTomaszewski(2018) , 'Energy-Optimal Data Aggregation and Dissemination for the Internet of Things' IEEE Internet of Things Journal, Vol.5, No. 2, Pp. 955 – 969

27. Evren G¨ uney, NecatiArasb, I. KubanAltınel , CemErsoy (2012), 'Efficient solution techniques for the integrated coverage, sink location and routing problem in wireless sensor networks' Computers &OperationsResearch, Vol.39, Pp.1530–1539

28. EvrenGüney, Necati Aras, I. Kuban Altınel, CemErsoy (2010), 'Efficient integer programming formulations for optimum sink location and routing in heterogeneous wireless sensor networks' Journal of Computer Networks- Elsevier,No. 54, pp.1805–1822

29. Fadi Al-Turjman, AymanRadwan (2017), 'Data Delivery in Wireless Multimedia Sensor Networks: Challenging and Defying in the IoT Era' IEEE Wireless Communications, Vol.24, No.5, pp. 126 – 131

30. Fadi M. Al-Turjman; Muhammad Imran; Sheikh Tahir Bakhsh (2017), 'Energy Efficiency Perspectives of Femtocells in Internet of Things: Recent Advances and Challenges' IEEE Access, Vol.5, pp. 26808 – 26818

31. Flammini, E. Sisinni(2014), 'Wireless sensor networking in the Internet of Things and cloud computing era', Proc. Eur. Conf. Solid-State Transducers (EUROSENSOR), Vol. 87, Pp. 672-679

32. Haojun Huang , Junbao Zhang , Xu Zhang, Benshun Yi , Qilin Fan , Feng Li(2017), 'EMGR: Energy-efficient multicast geographic routing in wireless sensor networks' Computer Networks, Vol. 129, Pp.51–63

33. Hussein Khayou, BakrSarakbi (2017), 'A validation model for non-lexical routing protocols', Journal of Network and Computer Applications-Elsevier, No.98, pp.58–64

34. Jian Li; Yun Liu; Zhenjiang Zhang; JianRen; Nan Zhao (2017),'Towards Green IoT Networking: Performance Optimization of Network Coding Based Communication and Reliable Storage' IEEE Access, Vol.5, Pp. 8780 - 8791

35. Jiang Q., V. C. M. Leung, M. T. Pourazad, H. Tang, H.-S. Xi (2016), 'Energy-efficient adaptive transmission of scalable video streaming in cognitive radio communications', IEEE Syst. J., Vol. 10, No. 2, pp. 761-772.

36. Jianguo Yao; Haihang Zhou; JianyingLuo; Xue Liu; Haibing Guan (2015), 'COMIC: Cost Optimization for Internet Content Multihoming' IEEE Transactions on Parallel and Distributed Systems, Vol.26,No. 7, pp. 1851 – 1860.

37. Jianli Pan; Raj Jain; Subharthi Paul; Chakchai So-in (2010), 'MILSA: A New Evolutionary Architecture for Scalability, Mobility, and Multihoming in the Future Internet' IEEE Journal on Selected Areas in Communications, Vol.28, No. 8, Pp. 1344 – 1362.

38. JianShen; Anxi Wang; Chen Wang; Patrick C. K. Hung; Chin-Feng Lai (2017) , 'An Efficient Centroid-Based Routing Protocol for Energy Management in WSN-Assisted IoT' IEEE Access, Vol.5, Pp. 18469 – 18479

39. Jiaxin Zeng; Yuanlong Cao; FenfenKe; Minghe Huang; Guanghe Zhang; Wei Lu (2018), 'Performance evaluation of secure multipath retransmission mechanism in next generation heterogeneous communication systems' IET Networks, Vol.7, No.2, Pp. 61 – 67

40. Jiyan Wu; Bo Cheng; Ming Wang; Junliang Chen (2016) , 'Delivering High-Frame-Rate Video to Mobile Devices in Heterogeneous Wireless Networks'IEEE Transactions on Communications, Vol.64, No.11, Pp. 4800 – 4816

41. Jongwook Lee; SaewoongBahk (2013), 'On the MDP-Based Cost Minimization for Video-on-Demand Services in a Heterogeneous Wireless Network with Multihomed Terminals', IEEE Transactions on Mobile Computing,Year: 2013, Vol.12, No. 9, Pp. 1737 – 1749

42. Joohyung Lee; Seonghwa Yun; Hyeontaek Oh; S. H. Shah Newaz; SeongGon Choi; Jun Kyun Choi (2016), 'Power-efficient rate allocation of wireless access networks with sleep-operation management for multihoming services' Journal of Communications and Networks, Vol.18,No.4,pp.619 – 628.

43. Jose Aguilar; Miguel A. Labrador (2007), 'A General Combinatorial Ant System-based Distributed Routing Algorithm for Communication Networks' IEEE Latin America Transactions, Vol.5, No.8, Pp. 616 – 625

44. Jose Flich; Tor Skeie; Andres Mejia; Olav Lysne; Pedro Lopez; Antonio Robles; Jose Duato; MichihiroKoibuchi; Tomas Rokicki; Jose Carlos Sancho (2012), 'A Survey and Evaluation of Topology-Agnostic Deterministic Routing Algorithms' IEEE Transactions on Parallel and Distributed Systems, Vol.23, No. 3, Pp. 405 – 425

45. Jun Huang; Cong-Cong Xing; Sung Y. Shin, Fen Hou; Ching-Hsien Hsu(2018), 'Optimizing M2M Communications and Quality of Services in the IoT for Sustainable Smart Cities' IEEE Transactions on Sustainable Computing, Vol.3, No.1, Pp. 4 - 15

46. Jun Huang; QiangDuan; Yanxiao Zhao; ZhongZheng; Wei Wang (2017), 'Multicast Routing for Multimedia Communications in the Internet of Things' IEEE Internet of Things Journal, Vol.4, No.1, Pp. 215 – 224

47. Junfei Huang; Zhaowen Lin (2017), 'Group-Aware Delay-Constrained Video Transmission Over Multihomed Device-to-Device Networks' IEEE Access, Year: 2017, Vol.5, Pp. 2651 - 2664

48. JunfengXu; Keqiu Li; Geyong Min (2012), 'Reliable and Energy-Efficient Multipath Communications in Underwater Sensor Networks' IEEE Transactions on Parallel and Distributed Systems, Vol.23, No.7, Pp. 1326 – 1335

49. Kaiyuan Yang; David Blaauw; Dennis Sylvester (2017), 'Hardware Designs for Security in Ultra-Low-Power IoT Systems: An Overview and Survey' IEEE Micro, Vol.37, No. 6, Pp. 72 – 89

50. Kisong Lee; Jun-Pyo Hong (2017), 'Power Control for Energy Efficient D2D Communication in Heterogeneous Networks with Eavesdropper' IEEE Communications Letters, Vol.21, No.11, pp. 2536 – 2539.

51. LapasPradittasnee; SeyitCamtepe; Yu-Chu Tian (2017), 'Efficient Route Update and Maintenance for Reliable Routing in Large-Scale Sensor Networks' IEEE Transactions on Industrial Informatics, Vol.13, No. 1, Pp. 144 – 156

52. Lei Xu; ArumugamNallanathan; Jian Yang; Wenhe Liao (2018), 'Power and Bandwidth Allocation for Cognitive Heterogeneous Multi-Homing Networks' IEEE Transactions on Communications, Vol.66, No.1, Pp.394 – 403

53. Li. X; Z. Jia; P. Zhang; R. Zhang; H. Wang (2010), 'Trust-based on-demand multipath routing in mobile ad hoc networks' IET Information Security, Vol.4, No. 4, Pp. 212 – 232

54. Liang Wang; Xiaohang Wang; Terrence Mak (2016), 'Adaptive Routing Algorithms for Lifetime Reliability Optimization in Network-on-Chip' IEEE Transactions on Computers, Vol.65, No.9, Pp. 2896 – 2902

55. Lichen Zhang; ZhipengCai; Peng Li; Liang Wang; Xiaoming Wang(2017), 'Spectrum-Availability Based Routing for Cognitive Sensor Networks,IEEE Access, Vol.5,Pp. 4448 – 4457

56. Liu Y.; N. Xiong; Y. Zhao; A. V. Vasilakos; J. Gao; Y. Jia (2010), 'Multi-layer clustering routing algorithm for wireless vehicular sensor networks' IET Communications, Vol. 4, No. 7, Pp. 810 – 816

57. Liumeng Song; KokKeong Chai; Yue Chen; John Schormans; Jonathan Loo; Alexey Vinel (2017), 'QoS-Aware Energy-Efficient Cooperative Scheme for Cluster-Based IoT Systems' IEEE Systems Journal, Vol.11, No.3, Pp. 1447 – 1455

58. Lizhong Chena, Di Zhub, MassoudPedramb, Timothy M. Pinkston (2016), 'Simulation of NoC power-gating: Requirements, optimizations, and the Agate simulator' Journal of . Parallel Distributed Computing, Vol. 95 , Pp.69–78

59. Lu Zhen, Shuaian Wang, Dan Zhuge (2017),'Analysis of three container routing strategies' International Journal of Production Economics, Vol. 193, Pp. 259–271

60. Luo J., L. Rao, X. Liu (2014), 'Temporal load balancing with service delay guarantees for data center energy cost optimization', IEEE Trans. Parallel Distrib. Syst., Vol. 25, No. 3, pp. 775-784.

61. Mahmoud HashemEiza; Thomas Owens; Qiang Ni (2016), 'Secure and Robust Multi-Constrained QoS Aware Routing Algorithm for VANETs', IEEE Transactions on Dependable and Secure Computing, Vol.13, No.1, Pp. 32 – 45

62. MalazKserawi; Sangsu Jung; Dujeong Lee; Jihoon Sung; June-Koo Kevin Rhee (2014) , 'Multipath Video Real-Time Streaming by Field-Based Anycast Routing' IEEE Transactions on Multimedia, Vol.16, No.2, Pp. 533 – 540

63. Manfredi S (2012), 'Reliable and energy-efficient cooperative routing algorithm for wireless monitoring systems' IET Wireless Sensor Systems, Vol.2, No. 2, Pp. 128 – 135

64. Manisekaran S.V, R. Venkatesan (2016), 'An analysis of software-defined routing approach for wireless sensor networks' journal of Computers and Electrical Engineering—Elsevier, No.56, pp. 456–467

65. Marc Barcelo, Alejandro Correa, Jaime Llorca, Antonia M. Tulino, Jose Lopez Vicario, AntoniMorell (2016), 'IoT-Cloud Service Optimization in Next Generation Smart Environments' IEEE Journal on Selected Areas in Communications, Vol. 34, No. 12, pp. 4077 – 4090

66. MargarethaGansterer, Richard F. Hartl (2017), 'Collaborative vehicle routing: A survey' European Journal of Operational Research Vol.1, Pp. 1–12

67. Marian Verhelst; Bert Moons (2017), 'Embedded Deep Neural Network Processing: Algorithmic and Processor Techniques Bring Deep Learning to IoT and Edge Devices' IEEE Solid-State Circuits Magazine, Vol.9, No.4, Pp. 55 – 65.

68. MasoumehEbrahimi (2013), 'Fully adaptive routing algorithms and region-based approaches for two-dimensional and three-dimensional networks-on-chip' IET Computers & Digital Techniques, Vol.7, No.6, Pp. 264 – 273

69. Maurizio Palesi; Rickard Holsmark; Shashi Kumar; Vincenzo Catania (2009), 'Application Specific Routing Algorithms for Networks on

Chip' IEEE Transactions on Parallel and Distributed Systems, Vol. 20, No.3, Pp. 316 – 330

70. Miguel Camelo; Carlos Omana; Harold Castro (2011), 'QoS Routing Algorithms based on Multi-Objective Optimization for Mesh Networks' IEEE Latin America Transactions,Vol.9, No. 5, Pp. 875 – 881

71. Mohammed ZakiHasan; Fadi Al-Turjman (2017), 'Optimizing Multipath Routing With Guaranteed Fault Tolerance in Internet of Things' IEEE Sensors Journal, Vol.17, No.19, Pp. 6463 – 6473

72. Mojahid Saeed Osman, Bala Ram (2017), 'Routing and scheduling on evacuation path networks using centralized hybrid approach' Computers and Operations Research, Vol. 88, Pp. 332–339.

73. Moraveji R.; P. Moinzadeh; H. Sarbazi-Azad; A. Y. Zomaya (2011), 'Multispanning Tree Zone-Ordered Label-Based Routing Algorithms for Irregular Networks' IEEE Transactions on Parallel and Distributed Systems, Vol.22, No.5, Pp. 817 – 832

74. Muhammad Ismail; WeihuaZhuang (2014), 'Mobile Terminal Energy Management for Sustainable Multi-Homing Video Transmission' IEEE Transactions on Wireless Communications, Vol.13, No. 8, Pp. 4616 – 4627

75. Muhammad Ismail; WeihuaZhuang; Samir Elhedhli (2013), 'Energy and Content Aware Multi-Homing Video Transmission in Heterogeneous Networks' IEEE Transactions on Wireless Communications, Vol.12, No.7, Pp. 3600 – 3610

76. Navroop Kaur; Sandeep K. Sood (2017), 'An Energy-Efficient Architecture for the Internet of Things (IoT)' IEEE Systems Journal, Vol.11, No.2,pp. 796 – 805.

77. Oladayo Bello; SheraliZeadally (2016), 'Intelligent Device-to-Device Communication in the Internet of Things' IEEE Systems Journal, Vol.10, No. 3, Pp. 1172 - 1182

78. Osama Alsaryrah; Ibrahim Mashal; Tein-Yaw Chung (2018), 'Bi-Objective Optimization for Energy Aware Internet of Things Service Composition' IEEE Access, Vol. 6, Pp. 26809 – 26819

79. Palesi M., Kumar S.; V. Catania (2009), 'Bandwidth-aware routing algorithms for networks-on-chip platforms' IET Computers & Digital Techniques, Vol.3, No. 5, Pp. 413 – 429

80. Perera C, A. Zaslavsky, P. Christen, and D. Georgakopoulos (2013), 'Context aware computing for the Internet of Things: A survey' IEEE Communication Surveys, Vol. 16, No. 1, pp. 414-454

81. Qin Yang; Sang-Jo Yoo (2018), 'ptimal UAV Path Planning: Sensing Data Acquisition Over IoT Sensor Networks Using Multi-Objective Bio-Inspired Algorithms' IEEE Access, Vol.6, Pp. 13671 – 13684

82. Quang-Doanh Vu; Le-Nam Tran; MarkkuJuntti; Een-Kee Hong (2015), 'Energy-Efficient Bandwidth and Power Allocation for Multi-Homing Networks' IEEE Transactions on Signal Processing, Vol.63, No.7, Pp.1684 – 1699

83. Raja Vara Prasad Yerra; M. P. R. S. Kiran; Rajalakshmi Pachamuthu (2015), 'Reliability and Delay Analysis of Slotted Anycast Multi-Hop Wireless Networks Targeting Dense Traffic IoT Applications' IEEE Communications Letters, Vol.19, No.5, Pp. 727 – 730

84. Rakesh Kumar Lenka; Amiya Kumar Rath; Zhiyuan Tan; Suraj Sharma; Deepak Puthal; N. V. R. Simha; Mukesh Prasad; Rohit Raja; Shankar SharanTripathi (2018), 'Building Scalable Cyber-Physical-Social Networking Infrastructure Using IoT and Low Power Sensors' IEEE Access, Vol. 6, Pp. 30162 – 30173

85. Romain Kuntz; Julien Montavont; Thomas Noel (2013), 'Multihoming in IPv6 mobile networks: progress, challenges, and solutions', IEEE Communications Magazine,Vol.51,No.1, pp.128 – 135.

86. Runzi Liu, Min Sheng, WeihuaWu(2018), 'Energy-Efficient Resource Allocation for Heterogeneous Wireless Network With Multi-Homed User Equipments',Vol.6,No.1,Pp.14591-14601.

87. SaiQian Zhang; Qi Zhang; HadiBannazadeh; Alberto Leon-Garcia (2015), 'Routing Algorithms for Network Function Virtualization Enabled Multicast Topology on SDN', IEEE Transactions on Network and Service Management, Vol.12, No.4, Pp. 580 – 594

88. SalimBitam; AbdelhamidMellouk; SheraliZeadally (2015) , 'Bio-Inspired Routing Algorithms Survey for Vehicular Ad Hoc Networks'IEEE Communications Surveys & Tutorials, Vol.17, No. 2, Pp. 843 – 867

89. Sandeep Kumar Singh; Tamal Das; AdmelaJukan (2015), 'A Survey on Internet Multipath Routing and Provisioning' IEEE Communications Surveys & Tutorials, Vol.17, No.4, Pp. 2157 – 2175

90. Satyam Agarwal; Swades De (2016), 'Cognitive Multihoming System for Energy and Cost Aware Video Transmission' IEEE Transactions on Cognitive Communications and Networking, Vol. 2, No.3,pp.316 – 329.

91. SelvakumarSasirekha; SankaranarayananSwamynathan (2017), 'Cluster-chain mobile agent routing algorithm for efficient data aggregation in wireless sensor network' Journal of Communications and Networks, Vol.19, No.4, Pp. 392 – 401

92. SemiyeDemircan, Musa Aydin ,S. SavasDurduran (2011), 'Finding optimum route of electrical energy transmission line using multi-criteria with Q-learning', Journal of Expert Systems with Applications- Elsevier,No.38,pp.3477–3482.

93. ShahramJamali, Leila Rezaei, SajjadJahanbakhshGudakahriz (2013), 'An Energy-efficient Routing Protocol for MANETs: a Particle Swarm Optimization Approach' Journal of Applied Research and Technology, Vol.11, pp.803-812.

94. SofianeHamrioui; Pascal Lorenz (2017), 'Bio Inspired Routing Algorithm and Efficient Communications within IoT' IEEE Network, Vol.31, No.5, Pp. 74 – 79

95. Sun Baolin; Li Layuan (2004), 'Optimizing on multiple constrained QoS multicast routing algorithms based on GA' Journal of Systems Engineering and Electronics, Vol.15, No. 4, Pp. 677 – 683

96. Sun Baolin; Li Layuan (2005), 'Multiple constraints-based QoS multicast routing: Model and algorithms' Journal of Systems Engineering and Electronics, Vol.16, No. 1, Pp. 187 – 193

97. Sungoh Kwon; Ness B. Shroff (2012), 'Energy-Efficient Unified Routing Algorithm for Multi-Hop Wireless Networks' IEEE Transactions on Wireless Communications, Vol.11, No.11, Pp. 3890 – 3899

98. SuvadipBatabyal; ParamaBhaumik (2015),'Mobility Models, Traces and Impact of Mobility on Opportunistic Routing Algorithms: A Survey' IEEE Communications Surveys & Tutorials, Vol.17, No. 3, Pp. 1679 – 1707

99. Swamy D. Ponpandi, AkhileshTyagi (2014), 'User satisfaction aware routing and energy modeling of polymorphic network on chip architecture' Computers and Electrical Engineering, Vol.40, Pp.260–275

100. TansuAlpcan; Jatinder Pal Singh; Tamer Başar (2009), 'Robust Rate Control for Heterogeneous Network Access in Multihomed Environments' IEEE Transactions on Mobile Computing, Vol. 8, No.1, Pp: 41 – 51

101. Tie Qiu; KaiyuZheng; Houbing Song; Min Han; BurakKantarci (2017), 'A Local-Optimization Emergency Scheduling Scheme With Self-Recovery for a Smart Grid' IEEE Transactions on Industrial Informatics, Vol.13, No. 6, Pp. 3195 – 3205

102. Ting Li; Jin Yuan; Murat Torlak (2018), 'Network Throughput Optimization for Random Access Narrowband Cognitive Radio Internet of Things (NB-CR-IoT)' IEEE Internet of Things Journal, Vol. 5, No. 3, Pp.1436 – 1448

103. Weihua Wu; Qinghai Yang; Bingbing Li; Kyung Sup Kwak (2016), 'Adaptive cross-layer resource optimization in heterogeneous wireless networks with multi-homing user equipments' Journal of Communications and Networks, Vol.18, No.5, Pp.784 – 795

104. Weihua Wu; Qinghai Yang; Peng Gong; Kyung Sup Kwak (2016), 'Energy-Efficient Resource Optimization for OFDMA-Based Multi-Homing Heterogenous Wireless Networks' IEEE Transactions on Signal Processing, Vol.64, No.22, Pp.5901 - 5913

105. Weihua Wu; Qinghai Yang; Peng Gong; Kyung Sup Kwak (2016), Adaptive Multi-Homing Resource Allocation for Time-Varying Heterogeneous Wireless Networks Without Timescale Separation, IEEE Transactions on Communications, Vol.64, No. 9, Pp. 3794 – 3807

106. Xiaoguang Zhang, Zheng Da Wu (2011), 'The balance of routing energy consumption in wireless sensor networks' Journal of . Parallel Distributed Computing. Vol.71, Pp. 1024–1033

107. Xiaojun Lin; Shahzada B. Rasool (2009), 'Distributed and Provably Efficient Algorithms for Joint Channel-Assignment, Scheduling, and Routing in Multichannel Ad Hoc Wireless Networks' IEEE/ACM Transactions on Networking, Vol.17, No.6, Pp. 1874 – 1887

108. Xiaomei Liu; Li Xiao (2007), 'A Survey of Multihoming Technology in Stub Networks: Current Research and Open Issues' IEEE Network, Vol.21, No.3, Pp.32 – 40.

109. Xiaomei Liu; Li Xiao (2010), 'ILBO: Balance Inbound Traffic Dynamically in Multihomed Stub Networks' IEEE Transactions on Parallel and Distributed Systems, Vol.21, No.11, Pp.1561 – 1572

110. Xiaomin Li; Di Li; Jiafu Wan; Chengliang Liu; Muhammad Imran (2018), 'Adaptive Transmission Optimization in SDN-Based Industrial Internet of Things With Edge Computing' IEEE Internet of Things Journal, Vol.5, No.3, Pp. 1351 – 1360

111. Xin Feng; Jing Zhang; ChenghaoRen; Tingting Guan (2018) , 'An Unequal Clustering Algorithm Concerned With Time-Delay for Internet of Things' IEEE Access, Vol.6, Pp. 33895 – 33909

112. Yanbin Sun, Yu Zhang, Binxing Fang, Hongli Zhang (2017), 'Succinct and practical greedy embedding for geometric routing' Journal of Computer Communications- Elsevier, Vol. 114, pp.51–61

113. YonganShu; ZiyuShu; Bin Luo (2014),'Incentive mechanism design for heterogeneous networking routing' Journal of Communications and Networks, Vol.16, No.4, Pp.458 – 464

114. Yosi Ben-Asher; Sharoni Feldman; Moran Feldman (2011), 'Dynamic Multipath Allocation in Ad Hoc Networks' The Computer Journal, Vol.54No. 2, Pp. 197 – 212

115. Yucen Nan; Wei Li; Wei Bao; Flavia C. Delicato; Paulo F. Pires; Yong Dou; Albert Y. Zomaya (2017), 'Adaptive Energy-Aware Computation Offloading for Cloud of Things Systems'IEEE Access, Vol.5, Pp. 23947 – 23957

116. Yuchao Chang; Hongying Tang; Baoqing Li; Xiaobing Yuan (2017), 'Distributed Joint Optimization Routing Algorithm Based on the Analytic Hierarchy Process for Wireless Sensor Networks' IEEE Communications Letters, Vol.21, No.12 , Pp. 2718 – 2721

117. Yujae Song; Yonghoon Choi; Youngnam Han (2018), 'Joint Optimization of Radio Resources for Uplink Multihoming Networks' IEEE Systems Journal, Vol.12, No. 1, Pp.671 – 681.

118. ZhezhuangXu; Liquan Chen; Cailian Chen; Xinping Guan (2016), 'Joint Clustering and Routing Design for Reliable and Efficient Data Collection in Large-Scale Wireless Sensor Networks' IEEE Internet of Things Journal, Vol.3, No.4, Pp. 520 – 532

119. Zihe Gao; Qing Guo; Zhenyu Na (2011), 'Novel optimized routing algorithm for LEO satellite IP networks' Journal of Systems Engineering and Electronics, Vol. 22, No. 6, Pp. 917 – 925

www.ingramcontent.com/pod-product-compliance
Lightning Source LLC
LaVergne TN
LVHW082350200926
848481LV00012B/3525
* 9 7 9 8 2 3 0 8 6 7 3 1 9 *